JOHN 1:1
AS PROOFTEXT

Trinitarian or Unitarian?

Garrett C. Kenney

University Press of America,® Inc.
Lanham • New York • Oxford

Copyright © 1999 by
University Press of America,® Inc.
4720 Boston Way
Lanham, Maryland 20706

12 Hid's Copse Rd.
Cumnor Hill, Oxford OX2 9JJ

Library of Congress Cataloging-in-Publication Data

Kenney, Garrett C.
John 1 : 1 as prooftext : Trinitarian or Unitarian? / Garrett C.
Kenney.
p.   cm.
Includes bibliographical references and indexes.
1. Bible. N.T. John I, 1—Theology. 2. Trinity—Biblical teaching.
3. Unitarianism—Biblical teaching. 4. Bible. N.T. John I, 1—
Criticism, interpretation, etc. I. Title.
BS2615.2.K37 1999   226.5'06—dc21   98-53598 CIP

ISBN 0-7618-1335-7 (pbk: alk. ppr.)

♾™ The paper used in this publication meets the minimum
requirements of American National Standard for Information
Sciences—Permanence of Paper for Printed Library Materials,

DEDICATION

To

Bruce Gore, mentor and friend

Contents

Preface

The focus of this book is the meaning of a single verse of the Bible, John 1:1. An attempt is made to determine whether or not this verse supports the doctrine of the trinity. The examination provided here takes the reader into the subtleties of several interpretive problems, balancing arguments on both sides of the debate. A conclusion is given in favor of a Trinitarian interpretation, but with an admission that the Unitarian position poses serious questions.

The methods of textual, lexical, grammatical, and translation criticism are explained and directly applied in a thorough manner to the interpretation of John 1:1. The methods of source, form, redaction, rhetorical, and composition criticism are explained but only partially and incompletely applied. There is certainly more to be learned and stated regarding the implications of John 1:1 as a prooftext for either Trinitarian or Unitarian views. Nevertheless, it is hoped that this work has provided a sound foundation for further investigation and dialogue by members of both interpretive parties.

Acknowledgements

The clarity of this manuscript is indebted to many helpful editorial suggestions from my two readers: Michael J. Kenney and Miriam J. Finnegan

Introduction

"In the beginning was the Word, and the Word was with God, and the Word was God." John begins his gospel with these familiar, frequently quoted words. But what did he mean by these words? Why did he choose to begin his gospel this way? How do these words "fit" with the other words of John's gospel? How do these words contribute to the overall fabric of Christian theology?

One purpose of this commentary is to answer these and other related questions. Another purpose is to illustrate HOW one goes about answering such questions. In other words, the focus of this commentary is upon both the MEANING of John 1:1 and the METHODS used to obtain a given interpretation.

Two competing interpretations have dominated the history of the interpretation of John 1:1. Trinitarians cite John 1:1 frequently and confidently as a prooftext for their view. The Word is understood as a reference to Jesus Christ who, in some mysterious manner, was with God, and was God, from the beginning of all time. In their view John 1:1 supplies scriptural support for the idea that God is one in three persons, the Father, Son, and Holy Spirit. Unitarians, however, are quick to point out that, upon closer inspection, John 1:1 does not yield such an interpretation, nor provide such support. This commentary will closely and carefully look at the details of John 1:1 in an attempt to dialogue with both groups. The goal will be an understanding of what the author of John 1:1 meant at the time of the original composition for the understanding of the original audience. Subsequent meanings (interpretations) can then be evaluated properly.

The approach of this commentary will be slow and systematic. John 1:1 will be examined from a variety of perspectives. Prior to beginning this arduous task are these few preliminary explanations: a) why this study is meaningful to its author; b) Trinitarian and Unitarian perspectives and presuppostions; and c) an overview of methodological approaches.

Why This Study Is Meaningful To Its Author

My father was a Roman Catholic, my mother a Christian Scientist. The former Trinitarian, the latter Unitarian. Mom reluctantly converted to Catholicism in order to proceed with her marriage. She often reminds me that her reluctant conversion came only after the second time through the required instructions (this was during the late 1940s). This marriage lasted 22 years. A divorce was granted. The lack of spiritual unity was not stated as a factor but may have contributed.

I was raised overtly Catholic, with Christian Science overtones. It has always been difficult to choose between Mom and Dad. This dilemma was compounded by a "conversion" experience which coincided with the trauma of my parent's divorce. My parent's lives were falling apart, our family was coming unglued, and I became acutely aware of the need for a Savior. I accepted Christ into my heart, started attending a local Pentecostal Church, read the scriptures incessantly, learned the habit of prayer, and began to notice the quality of my life improving.

The previous two paragraphs telescope the first two decades of my life. The next two provide a synopsis of the subsequent two decades. These provide the reader with some insight as to why this research is meaningful to me.

Some converts to Christianity remain in the same denomination all their lives. Others navigate their way through several in hopes of finding a home. I am one of the latter. My search fluctuated between Trinitarian and Unitarian groups, perhaps a reflection of my upbringing. Throughout my involvement with these groups I was actively involved in teaching, primarily in adult education. My early and successful "Sunday school" teaching experience contributed to my effectiveness as a college professor. For the past 20 years I have taught humanities and religion courses for several universities in the Pacific Northwest.

Throughout my teaching career I have wrestled with the debate between Trinitarianism and Unitarianism. This issue is inescapable when one is repeatedly assigned courses on first century Judaism, the historical Jesus, New Testament, Church history, and world religions. The complexity of this topic has been impressed upon me as I have labored to trace the historical, philosophical, and scriptural bases of Trinitarian and Unitarian perspectives. This commentary on John 1:1 provides an opportunity to clarify, both for myself and for my readers, how this one verse is understood within the context of this debate.

Trinitarian and Unitarian Perspectives and Presuppostions

In this section I will offer a definition of Trinitarianism and Unitarianism along with definitions of key terms. A few of the representative presuppositions and perspectives of both schools of thought will be identified. A few comments will be made with regard to some of the biblical "prooftexts" called upon by each school of thought to support its position.

Unitarianism may be defined as follows: the belief that God is one substance and one person, the Father. The Son (Jesus Christ) is not God as the Father is God. The Holy Spirit (holy spirit) is a synonym for the Father, who is Holy and who is Spirit. The Father gives holy spirit (an impersonal gift, or empowerment) to those who believe. The preceeding definition may not represent all forms of Unitarianism but it does contain the essential point common to all forms of this view. The essential point being this: Jesus is NOT God in the same sense that God the Father is God.

Trinitarianism may be defined as follows: God is one substance consisting of three intrinsic and interrelated persons, Father, Son, and Holy Spirit. Each person is as fully God as the other, but not without the other(s). The essential point in this view, for the purposes of understanding John 1:1, is that Jesus is understood as true God of true God. Jesus, in Trinitarian understanding, is as much God as God the Father is God. The traditional term adopted to express this concept is the Greek term ὁμουσια (homousia). It is NOT a biblical term, but in the view of Trinitarians it captures the meaning of what the Bible says, particularly John 1:1.

Key to the debate over Trinitarianism and Unitarianism are the terms "person" and "substance." These two terms have a rich and complicated history, especially during the first four centuries of the development of Christian thought. It is beyond the scope of this commentary to given adequate exposition to the varied and subtle nuances of these terms. Thus, they are defined here in brief. Person may refer to: that aspect of a being which involves rights and obligations due to self-awareness, creativity, imagination, and independent-exclusive (or interdependent- inclusive) volition. The key terms used in the early history of the development of this concept were prosopon (Latin) and ὑποστασις (hypostasis: Greek). Substance may refer to: that aspect of a being which constitutes its essential nature, attributes, and characteristics. For example, in the case of God, substance consists of such attributes as: ubiquity; omnipotence; omniscience; omnibenevolence; eternality; holiness; etc. The key term used for this concept in the early church was the Greek term οὐσια (ousia). The point to be noted for the focus of this commentary is this: Trinitarian interpreters maintain that John 1:1 provides a scriptural basis for both the distinction of persons within the Godhead (at least with regard to the Father and the Word/Son) and their equality as God. Unitarian interpreters maintain that John 1:1 provides no such support.

At this point it may be helpful to comment upon some of the presuppositions and perspectives that Trinitarians and Unitarians often bring to their study of John 1:1. Most of my readers are probably prejudiced in their view of John 1:1 in one direction or another. Considering how the other side may be viewing or approaching the text is undertaken here in an ecumenical spirit. Understanding, sensitivity, respect, and dialogue are considered the goals here.

Unitarians honor the authority of the Bible. They believe that the Bible is an inspired revelation of God and thus profitable for doctrine, reproof, and correction. This should explain why a discussion of John 1:1 often generates as much heat as light. The interpretation of a text so vital to the understanding of the central figure (Jesus) of Christianity is not likely to be set aside lightly, or allowed to be interpreted to anyone's fancies or whims. Unitarians, in their approach to John 1:1, invoke a sound principle of biblical interpretation. They insist that an obscure, ambiguous, or unclear text needs to be interpreted in light of several clear, more straightforward texts. This principle is offered in the interest of upholding the simplicity and consistency of the biblical revelation. What is said in one place should cohere with what is said in another. Hence, passages which clearly state that there is only one God, or that this one God is the Father, need to be impressed upon any interpreter of John 1:1 who would construe the verse to teach otherwise. Among passages cited are (King James Version throughout, unless otherwise noted): 1 Corinthians 8:6, "For unto us there is one God, the Father. . ."; 1 Timothy 2:5, "For there is one God and one mediator between God and man, himself a man, Christ Jesus"; and, John 17:3, "That they may know thee (the Father) , the only true God".

Some brief comments may be helpful here. 1 Corinthians 8:6 does clearly identify the one God as the Father. 1 Timothy does not specify the one God as the Father, but neither is Jesus referred to as God in this verse; rather he is referred to as the human mediator between God and man. John 17:3 is found in the context of Jesus' high priestly prayer. Here Jesus, addressing his Father (clearly stated in John 17:2) in prayer, refers to Him as the only true God. Hence, according to Unitarians, and based upon the principle of biblical interpretation stated above, John 1:1 needs to be interpreted in such a way that it harmonizes with these other verses. Essential to the fervor of Unitarian thought is their effort to uphold monotheism. Since the Bible so clearly teaches that there is only one God, the Father, other views, such as the Trinitarian view, are considered a move in the direction of polytheism.

Trinitarians also honor the authority of the Bible. They believe that the Bible is an inspired revelation of God and thus profitable for doctrine, reproof, and correction. Discussions of John 1:1 are often emotionally charged. Although certain that John 1:1 supports a Trinitarian understanding of God, many Trinitarian interpreters are not clear as to why or how. Hence, discussions with Unitarians on this verse usually make little progress. This commentary is written in an attempt to provide a bridge of understanding for both sets of interpreters to cross. The focus here is upon the factual details of the text in question in light of the application of appropriate methodologies. But first, a few more words with regard to Trinitarian presuppositions.

Trinitarians invoke a different principle of hermeneutics than do Unitarians. Rather than the difficult verse being interpreted in light of the clear verse they insist that sometimes the integrity of the difficult verse (such as John 1:1) requires the clear verse(s) to be set aside, or at least qualified. Comprehensiveness, not simplicity, is the goal of interpretation in their view. Any theory in any field of study is judged by its negotiation of the tension between simplicity and comprehensiveness. Theories should remain as simple as possible in light of their ability to comprehend, or explain, the data. But, when the data is not receiving adequate treatment, or being upheld in its integrity, then theories need to get a little more sophisticated. Such is the reasoning of Trinitarians. The following citations of often quoted prooftexts provide illustration: Matthew 28:19 states, "Go ye into all the world making disciples of all nations, baptizing them in the name of the Father, and of the Son, and of the Holy Spirit. . ."; 2 Corinthians 13:14 states, "Now the grace of our Lord Jesus Christ, and the love of God, and the fellowship of the Holy Spirit be with you all"; and, John 20:28 states, "And Thomas said unto him [Jesus], My Lord and My God".

These verses, like John 1:1, do not clearly teach a Trinity. But it is difficult to dismiss them too quickly. Interpreters do need to pay attention to details. Matthew 28:19 mentions three but with a singular name. Is the integrity of this verse upheld by insisting that the Holy Spirit (holy spirit) is not a person here? Why would two persons be mentioned with an impersonal gift and all comprehended by one name? Certainly the trinity is not proved, but the details of the text demand some reflection and explanation. Likewise, 2 Corinthians 13:14 mentions three, two of these clearly being persons, the Father and the Son. But why mention the Holy Spirit (holy spirit) in such a context if the Holy Spirit (holy spirit) is not an equal person with the others? Especially in the context of a liturgical blessing! John 20:28 is closer to the concerns and context of John 1:1. John 20:28 portrays Thomas addressing Jesus as "Lord" and "God." Significant here is the presence of the definite article (ὁ, ho, in Greek; "the" in English) missing before "God" (θεός, theos, in Greek) in the third clause of John 1:1. Trinitarians often argue that John 20:28 constitutes an inclusion with John 1:1, allowing one to interpret the anarthrous theos of John 1:1 in light of the arthrous theos in John 20:28. The import of this will be fully discussed in Chapter Three.

The reader is now aware that a detailed discussion of one verse often involves a detailed discussion of several related verses. Efforts will be made in this commentary to give full attention to John 1:1 and to reduce the focus from the related verses. But the preceeding paragraph illustrates some of the difficulty of this task. The main point here is that Trinitarians do not quickly yield to the so called clear verses. The integrity of each verse demands careful scrutiny. Ideally, all verses should be harmonized, but not at the expense of their integrity. For Trinitarians it is the Unitarians who are polytheists. For while they insist that there is only one God, the Father, they are confronted with texts which may teach otherwise. In addition, early Christians were characterized as those who gave utmost devotion to Jesus (cf. Bauckham, 1980/81).

In summary, the issue between Trinitarians and Unitarians is not the divine inspiration of the Bible. Both groups honor the authority of the Bible and base their views upon what they believe to be the correct interpretation of the biblical data. In general, Trinitarians and Unitarians differ in their hermeneutical emphasis. One puts emphasis upon the simple and clear texts, interpreting the obscure in light of the clear. The other puts an emphasis upon the integrity of the details of apparently unclear texts, attempting a comprehensive accounting of the data of the biblical revelation. Both groups charge the other with polytheism. Both groups have their lists of prooftexts. John 1:1 features prominently in the debate. This commentary investigates the meaning of John 1:1 according to procedural methods recognized as valid by both Trinitarians and Unitarians. An overview of these methods is now provided in order to give the reader a sense of the plan and approach of this commentary.

An Overview of Methodological Approaches

This final section provides an overview of the methods to be used. Of the numerous methods at the disposal of the modern interpreter only nine have been directly chosen for comment. It is my conviction that the task of interpretation is ongoing; even though nine methods are consciously selected, various other methods will come into play indirectly. This will become clear in the following overview.

Each of the nine methods will be defined and explained in brief. A more detailed explanation of steps, rules, and criteria appears in the individual chapters of a given method. The order in which these methods are identified represents the order of the chapters in this commentary. A rationale for this order will be provided.

Where does one start the process of interpretation? Does one step logically preceed another? Both of these questions deserve clear answers. The process of interpretation begins with one's first encounter with the text. My advice is to read the text and immediately record one's first impressions. These impressions often contain good questions and insights, but may reflect one's bias as well. Second, third, fourth, and subsequent readings help answer questions, refine insights, and eliminate or confirm one's bias. John 1:1 should be read afresh in its context (I suggest John 1:1-18, or the first chapter) and questions, comments, or insights should be recorded. Does it teach that Jesus is God? Does it not teach this? Why? What evidence is found for either assertion? If the reader has participated in this exercise then an explanation of the following steps can be appreciated as a guide to the more detailed and serious study that will take place in the subsequent chapters.

Interpretation of a given text may begin with an analysis of the text itself or with an analysis of information from another vantage point. This concept is known as the hermeneutical (interpretive) circle. In general the principle is stated as follows: Interpretation proceeds from the part to the whole or from the whole to the part. In particular the principle is understood as follows: interpretation proceeds from the text in question to particular vantage points or from particular vantage points to the text in question. Interpretation is refined by this process. This commentary applies this concept to John 1:1.

John 1:1 is the first part of the gospel of John. In this study John 1:1 is referred to as the target text, the focus of interpretation. The whole of John 1:1 includes the document which contains John 1:1, that is, the gospel of John, and a whole lot more. There are numerous vantage points. Another way of referring to the whole, or these numerous vantage points, is context. Context may be immediate or remote. For example, the immediate context of John 1:1 could be considered John 1:1-5, or John 1:1-18, or the whole first chapter. The remote context might be John chapters 2-12, or 2-21, or the whole gospel. Context is also understood as internal or external. The internal context refers to the parameters of the immediate and remote contexts just suggested. External context would include works by the same author, or those within a similar school of thought. This would include the epistles of John and the book of Revelation. These works are contained in the New Testament. Hence, the entire New Testament canon should be considered for its bearing upon John 1:1. One might now imagine the circle of context to widen.

The New Testament canon is clearly conceived as an extension of the Old Testament canon. Several of the New Testament documents begin with an invocation of the authority of the Old Testament (cf. Matthew 1:1-18; Mark 1:1-4; Romans 1:1-4; Hebrews 1:1-4). The Gospel of John is no exception. John 1:1, "In the beginning . . . ," clearly echoes Genesis 1:1. And the widening of the circle continues. Writings which are similar to or influential upon or important for the interpretation of Old and New Testament texts need to be considered. The following selected list illustrates just how extensive these writings may be: The Aramaic Targums; the Septuagint; the Apocrypha; the Pseudepigrapha; the Dead Sea Scrolls; the writings of Philo of Alexandria; the Talmud and Midrashim; Greco-Roman literary and philosophical classics; the Mystery Religions; Gnostic literature; and the Apostolic and Church Fathers. Relevant selections of these texts are often compiled into a single reference work. Recommended is *The New Testament background: Selected documents*, by C. K. Barrett (1987). Finally, external context includes research into the historical and cultural worlds of these texts. The interpretation of John 1:1, or any other ancient text for that matter, is no small task.

So, where does this commentary begin? Of the two extreme starting points, the target text (John 1:1), or its widest external context (say the Aramaic Targums or the Church Fathers), this commentary has chosen the target text itself. Hence, we will "hug" the text of John 1:1, staying as close to home as possible, but without forgetting the importance of the hermeneutical circle.

The nine methods selected for comment are: (1) textual; (2) lexical; (3) grammatical; (4) rhetorical; (5) translation; (6) form; (7) source; (8) redaction; and (9) composition criticism. Each of these will now be briefly defined and explained. A rationale for their order is also provided.

Textual criticism seeks to establish the original text. Obviously, if one has the original there is no need for this method. However, such is not the case with the gospel of John. Only copies exist, and these in abundance. Recommended on the history of the transmission of the text of the gospel of John is *The Fourth Gospel: A history of the text,* by Victor Salmon (1976). The earliest witness, Manchester papyrus 457, dates to about 125 C. E., within decades of the plausible composition of the gospel of John (cf. Salmon, 1976, 44). Other manuscripts date from the mid-second century through the sixteenth century. The science of textual criticism evaluates the authenticity of the several witnesses in an attempt to reconstruct the original. In the case of John 1:1 there are some interesting variant readings. A decision needs to be made as to the original reading of this verse. Wisdom dictates that one decide on the authentic content of a text prior to interpreting it. Hence, the rationale for this first step.

Lexcial criticism seeks to establish an accurate understanding of the meaning of the individual words found in the target text. These words, in the case of John 1:1, were originally written in Greek, with possible Hebrew and Aramaic influence. Hence, these backgrounds will need to be investigated. Having established the original words (step 1), establishing their correct meaning is in order (step 2).

Grammatical criticism seeks to establish an accurate understanding of the relationships between and among words. Here one identifies subject, verb, object and possible modifiers. If there is more than one clause, as is the case in John 1:1, then the relationship between clauses needs to be understood. Logically, this third step picks up where steps 1 and 2 leave off.

Rhetorical criticism, as defined in this commentary, focuses upon the figurative use of language. Communication may be literal, figurative, or a combination of both. This step identifies where, when, and how the communication departs from the literal. This is an important additional step to the three preceeding in that it directs the reader's attention to the intended emphasis of the thought expressed. Recommended here is *Figures of speech used in the Bible*, by E. W. Bullinger (1968).

Introduction

Translation criticism seeks to establish an appropriate rendition of the target text from the original language (Greek) into the receptor language (English). I say "appropriate rendition" because translation theories range between an emphasis upon faithfulness to the ancient form to an emphasis upon contemporary relevance (cf. Bolich, 1986, 81-95). In the chapter on translation criticism several translations representing the emphases of the continuum just mentioned will be considered. Steps 1, 2, 3, and 4 appear as prerequisites to step 5. One needs to know the authentic content, the meanings of the words, the grammar of the words, and possible figures of speech prior to translating. One desires a clear and competent translation before preceeding too deeply into a discussion of the meaning of a verse. Hence, the rationale for the location of this step.

Form criticism seeks to identify the literary form or genre of the target text. This step aids in classifying the target text according to a known literary form, which, by analogy with other such forms, provides guidance for a correct understanding. In addition, a comparison of the target text with other texts of similar form may reveal the innovations of the author of the target text.

Source criticism seeks to identify the presence or influence of external documents in the composition of the target text. In this step one considers the relationship of John 1:1, in its immediate context as a part of the prologue of John's gospel (1:1-18), to its relationship to the gospel as a whole. In addition, passages parallel in thought or wording to John 1:1 are considered.

Redaction criticism seeks to articulate an author's use of sources. In this step, the interests, uses, and motives for an author's use of sources are identified. Obviously, this step is logically subsequent to source criticism.

Composition criticism seeks to ascertain the meaning of the target text within the parameters of its internal context. Hence, the relationship of John 1:1 to discernible units of context, both immediate and remote, is in focus in this step.

These nine steps provide a foundation for further study. As the concept of the hermeneutical circle suggests, an almost endless series of steps could follow. Although limited in explanation to nine steps this commentary will indirectly suggest several other steps. Key to the strategy of this commentary are the following beliefs about the process of interpretation: (1) interpretation is refined in and through the process of the "steps" of the hermeneutical circle; (2) these steps, although focused upon one at a time, are, in reality, simultaneously in operation; (3) the science of interpretation, governed as it is by "rules," is also an art; interpretive conclusions do vary; and, (4) the task of interpretation is ongoing; conclusions arrived at are only as strong as the weakest link in the chain.

Chapter One

John 1:1 and Textual Criticism

This chapter will look at John 1:1 in light of the method of textual criticism. We will begin with the facts, a listing of the ancient witnesses. This will be followed by an explanation of the method, its theory and principles. As we proceed we will look at the possible variants of John 1:1 in light of the method. We will conclude with a decision about the original contents of our target text.

Several resources are available to the person interested in reconstructing the original contents of a given verse of the New Testament (NT). The most helpful resource for observing the bulk of textual information for the Gospel of John is Reuben Swanson's *New Testament manuscripts: Variant readings arranged in horizontal lines against Codex Vaticanus* (1995). Helpful resources for understanding the theory and principles by which data is interpreted are the following: Bruce Metzger's *A textual commentary on the Greek New Testament* (1971); Gregory G. Bolich's *The Christian scholar: An introduction to theological research* (1986, 96-112); and Jack Finegan's *Encountering New Testament manuscripts: A working introduction to textual criticism* (1974). These, and other resources, have been consulted for the analysis of this chapter.

According to Swanson (1995) all Greek manuscripts (mss.) agree on the contents of John 1:1, except one. This is an uncial manuscript (ms.) referred to as Codex Regius, or more briefly as ms. L 019, dated approximately in the eight century. The ms. is located in Paris (Swanson, 1995, vii). A. T. Robertson states that this ms. is "badly written" (1925, 89). Metzger (1971, xxix) and Finegan (1974, 74) classify this ms. in the later Alexandrian family. This

1

ms. differs from all others by the presence of one word, a word consisting of a single letter.

The first line below represents the Greek text of John 1:1 as it appears in all other mss., except L 019. The second line presents the reading of L 019, highlighting in ***bold italics*** the single lettered word that distinguishes it from all other witnesses. Below these two lines I have provided a transliteration of the previous Greek texts in order that my readers who are unfamiliar with Greek script can pronounce it in English. This will serve as the pronunciation guide for the Greek text of John 1:1 for the remainder of the commentary. Below these lines I have provided a simple word for word translation.

ἐν ἀρχῃ ἦν ὁ λογος, και ὁ λογος ἦν προς τον θεον, και θεος ἦν ὁ λογος

L 019

ἐν ἀρχῃ ἦν ὁ λογος, και ὁ λογος ἦν προς τον θεον,και *ὁ* θεος ἦν ὁ λογος

en arche ayn ho logos, και ho logos ayn pros ton theon, και theos ayn ho logos

L 019

en arche ayn ho logos, και ho logos ayn pros ton theon, και *ho* theos ayn ho logos

In beginning was the Word, and the Word was with the God, and God was the Word.

L 019

In beginning was the Word, and the Word was with the God, and *the* God was the Word.

The difference between L 019 and all other witnesses is the presence of the word ὁ (ho, the). An explanation of the significance of this difference will be given in the discussion below.

One might be tempted to dismiss ms. L 019 on the basis that it is a late ms., the only one with this variant, and judged by one expert (A. T. Robertson) to be "badly written." But this is to come to a conclusion prematurely. Good scholarship requires that conclusions are reached by sifting through data in a systematic and methodical manner. This lonely variant will be rejected for the reasons just given, plus others. But, since the focus of this commentary is upon method, as well as meaning, an explanation of the theory and principles of textual criticism will be provided. In this way the dismissal of ms. L 019 can be appreciated with greater confidence.

Bolich defines textual criticism as "the study of copies of a work with the aim of ascertaining the original text" (1986, 95). There are no original mss. for any of the books of the NT, which of course includes John's gospel. There are, however, plenty of copies. These copies are categorized into text-types and families. Among the text-types are the uncial and cursive codices (books) and the papyri scrolls. A codex is a ms. in book form. A papyrus ms. consists of sheets of paper (made from the papyrus reed) glued together so as to be rolled into a scroll. Uncials are mss. written in ALL CAPITAL letters. Cursives are mss. written in all small letters. Mss. are conveniently divided into four families: The Alexandrian; Western; Caesarean; and Byzantine (cf. Bolich, 1986,103-04).

According to Victor Salmon (1976, 7) there are 2, 754 cursive mss., 266 uncial mss., and 81 papyri. In addition to these witnesses are early translations of the gospel of John into languages other than the original Greek (e.g., Latin, Coptic, Syriac, Ethiopian). All these versions support the majority reading of John 1:1 against ms. L 019. Then there are lectionaries and patristic quotations. A lectionary is a book containing short excerpts of the NT selected and arranged for liturgical reading. These lectionary readings were copied from available mss. of the NT and hence provide additional witness to the (possible) original reading. All lectionary readings support the majority reading of John 1:1 against ms. L 019. Patristic quotations are found in the writings of the early Church Fathers (patris is Latin for father). These early Christian theologians, in promulgating their ideas, often quoted the NT from an available text or from memory (much like today). These quotations are so numerous that almost the entire NT could be reconstructed from them (cf. Bolich, 1986, 98). Hence, these quotations provide another valuable resource for textual criticism.

The patristic quotations also support the majority reading of John 1:1, at least with regard to the question of "God" versus "the God" in the final clause of John 1:1. There are, however, some variations in the quotations of other portions of John 1:1. For example, Clement of Alexandria (c.155-c.220), when quoting John 1:1, gives these variations: ". . . the Word *who* was with God," and ". . . the Word was *in* God," in place of "the Word was with God" (cf. Swanson, 1995, 5). These variations, when analyzed in context, appear more as commentary, elaborations, interpretations, or paraphrases rather than direct quotations (these have been checked by using the indices of the multi-volume series *The Ante-Nicene Fathers*). Further evidence for this is the fact that when Clement cites John 1:1, as an apparent quotation, rather than as elaboration, he does so in harmony with the majority reading of John 1:1.

Sifting through this mass of evidence is an enormous task. Robertson states, ". . . it is not possible for anyone to claim intimate knowledge of this vast collection of manuscripts" (1925, 69). Yet, through the help of concordances, indices, and other references to these resources, one is able to at least gain reasonable clarity on one verse (e.g., John 1:1).

In an attempt to reconstruct the original text of John 1:1 scholars first look at the internal evidence, then the external evidence, and then evaluate their findings. Internal evidence " is that material within a reading that reflects the probability of scribal change" (Bolich, 1986, 99). Scribes may have altered the text from which they were copying either intentionally or unintentionally. Unintentional errors may be of sight, sound, or memory. For example, scribes could have added or omitted the questionable ὁ (ho, the) of John 1:1c in any of these ways. Intentional "errors" reflect judgments by scribes that the text from which they were copying was wrong. These judgments could be based on a decision to correct grammar, spelling, or doctrine.

With regard to our target text, the presence or absence of the ὁ , on purely grammatical grounds, is acceptable either way. The presence of ὁ would convey that the God and the Word were synonymous, interchangeable, and completely identical terms (cf. Robertson, 1934, 767-68). An instructive example of this construction is close at hand. John 1:4 reads as follows:

και *ἡ* ζωη ἠν *το* φως
και *he* zoe ayn *to* phos
and *the* life was *the* light

Here life and light are interchangeable terms. The author of the gospel of John appears to be quite aware of the convertible use of the article, as this, and other potential examples, make clear. But, the absence of ὁ in John 1:1c is not only grammatically acceptable, it is contextually preferable. The previous clause of John 1:1, "and the Word was with the God," makes a clear distinction between God and the Word. Although an equation between God and the Word in John 1:1c is technically possible (as made clear by the example in John 1:4), the immediate context demands otherwise. John 1:1c is 'sandwiched' between two clauses which make a clear distinction between God and the Word. The following illustration makes this clear:

John 1:1b: και ὁ λογος ἠν προς τον θεον
and the Word was with the God
(God and the Word distinguished)

John 1:1c: και θεος ἠν ὁ λογος
and God was the Word (the relation qualified somehow)

John 1:2: οὑτος ἠν ἐν αρχη προς τον θεον
this one was in beginning with the God
(God and the Word distinguished)

The remote context is consistent with this point as well! Throughout the prologue (John 1:1-18) a distinction is maintained between God and the Word (seen very clearly in verses 1:1b, 2, 14, and 18). Hence, the intrinsic probability of the reading suggested by ms. L 019 is unlikely on the grounds of internal consistency. It appears to me as either an unintentional error, due to sight or sound (και ὁ does begin the second clause of John 1:1 and could be mistaken for the start of the third clause, which begins with και as well), or an intentional but ignorant blunder. The correct reading of the third clause of John 1:1, in my judgment, is "God" without the ὁ. Hence, God and the Word, in John 1:1c, are related to each other in a qualified, rather than in an absolute manner. This qualification is critical to the Trinitarian and Unitarian debate and will be fully discussed in Chapter Three.

Now, regarding the external evidence for the variants of John 1:1. Scholars have devised general principles to guide their decisions here. Bolich (1986, 104) suggests the following: (1) a text of the Alexandrian family is generally the most reliable; (2) when two of the most reliable Alexandrian texts (Codex Vaticanus and Codex Sinaiticus) agree on a given reading it is given preference; but, (3) a reading strongly supported by two or more text-types generally is preferable to the witness of any one text-type by itself; and, (4) where manuscripts within a text-type disagree, the preferred reading (as the one best representative of the text-type) is the one generally most consonant with that text-type, and different from the other text-types. These principles must be evaluated in conjunction with observations based on the internal evidence. We can now begin to draw conclusions regarding the original contents of John 1:1.

Only one ms. differs in its rendering of John 1:1, that is Codex Regius, L 019, of the later Alexandrian text-type. Although qualifying for consideration on the basis of principle #1 (above) it would be disqualified on the basis of the remaining three principles. Neither Codex Vaticanus nor Codex Sinaiticus agree with Codex Regius, thus disqualifying Codex Regius on the basis of principles #2 and #4 above. All three of the other text-types disagree against Codex Regius, thus disqualifying it also on principle #3 above. Reasons for rejecting the variant of Codex Regius can now be summarized:

1. Codex Regius fails to merit consideration on the basis of 3 of the 4 major principles of external evidence;

2. All lectionary readings, translations (versions), and patristic quotations (considered in context) support the majority reading against this variant;

3. On the basis of internal evidence the variant suggested is unlikely. It is not consonant with the style, vocabulary, or context of the gospel of John in its portrayal of the relationship between God and the Word, with or without the article. (This observation will receive fuller treatment in Chapter Three). And;

4. At least one expert (A. T. Robertson) deems this ms. to be "badly writ-

ten." No doubt there are others who concur. It is of interest to note that major commentaries do not even mention this variant (e.g.: Barrett, 1978; Brown, 1966; Bultmann, 1971; Dodd, 1963; Haenchen, 1980; Hoskyns, 1947; Kysar, 1976; Lightfoot, 1956; Lindars, 1981; Morris, 1971; and, Schnackenburg, 1982)!

The first step of the quest for understanding John 1:1 is now complete. The original contents of John 1:1 have been established on the basis of the recognized principles of textual criticism. Certainly more could be learned about Codex Regius, L 019 and textual criticism. Corrections and refinements are always welcome. These keep the wheels of scholarship rolling. Before reading the next chapter the reader is encouraged to review the four beliefs about the process of interpretation stated in the Introduction (page xv).

Chapter Two

John 1:1 and Lexical Criticism

This chapter will look at John 1:1 in light of the method of lexical criticism. The goal of lexical criticism is an understanding of the *basic* meaning of the words under investigation. The standard dictionaries for an understanding of New Testament Greek are: Thayer (1885); Bullinger (1887); Moulton & Milligan (1930); Arndt & Gingrich (1957); Liddel & Scott (1966); Kittel & Friedrich (1964-74); and, Brown (1975-78). In addition to lexicons the major commentaries and several specialized studies are recommended. Especially helpful for the results of this chapter were: Dodd (1954); Lovelady (1963); Mickelsen (1963); Beekman & Callow (1974); Terry (1974); Dunn (1980); and Erickson (1987).

The method of lexical criticism stops short of both translation and interpretation and needs to be distinguished from these subsequent steps. In translation an effort is made to go beyond the basic meaning of a given word in order to provide a more readable sense of a passage in light of authorial style and context. Translation begins the process of interpretation. Interpretation builds upon translation and provides further refinement through the exposition and elaboration of a myriad of details. For example, ἐν ἀρχη, the first two words of John 1:1, basically mean, "in the beginning." But, translators, wanting to make it clear that John's context involves a reference to the Genesis creation of the world (cf. John 1:3-5), might choose to translate these first two words: "at the start of the creation of the world." Interpreters, in expositing and elaborating upon this phrase, might speculate about when this creation took place and whether or not there may have been creations prior to the one spoken of in Genesis. This commentary will return to these considerations of translation and interpretation. Establishing the basic meaning of each of the words of John 1:1 is preliminary.

In order to accomplish the task of this chapter an inventory of the words of John 1:1 is needed. This will be followed by an explanation of the method of lexical criticism. There are 17 words in John 1:1, but only 8 are unique, as several words are repeated a number of times. Hence, the goal of this chapter is to identify the basic meaning of each of the 8 unique words. A presentation of John 1:1, identifying the unique words as they appear, will help the reader focus upon and identify which words will be investigated.

> John 1:1:
> ἐν[1] ἀρχν [2] ἦν [3] ὁ [4] λογος,[5] και [6] ὁ λογος ἦν προς [7] τον θεον,[8] και θεος ἦν ὁ λογος.

These 8 unique words are indicated above and footnoted below. The repeated words are: ὁ (4x; τον is a grammatical inflection of ὁ); λογος (3x); ἦν (3x); and θεος (2x; θεον is a grammatical inflection of θεος).

How does one determine the basic meaning of a given word? Among suggested guidelines in lexical criticism are the following: (1) identify the etymology, origin, or semantic components; (2) identify the history of usage, especially noting transitions in meaning; (3) identify synonyms and antonyms in order that related and opposite meanings are distinguished; and, (4) note the specific ways in which a given author may communicate meaning through subject matter, context, consistent usage, varied usage, and expressed or implied definition (cf. Mickelsen, 1963, 117-29; Beekman & Callow, 1974, 67-79; and Terry, 1974, 175-90). These guidelines will now be applied to the 8 unique words of John 1:1.

1. ἐν: This small word is a preposition with a long history. In Homeric times it was variously spelled as εἰν, ἐνι, εἰνι, or, ἐνς. Originally, this preposition indicated rest within or motion toward a person, place, or thing. In time the connotation of motion toward was taken over by the preposition εἰς. Yet, the distinction between ἐν and εἰς was not always, or consistently, observed. A variety of nuances came to be associated with ἐν. It has been called a "maid of all work" (Robertson, 1934, 586). In English translation it is rendered as "in, on, at, with, by, among" (Thayer, 1885, 209). In the NT it is the most frequently used of all prepositions (2, 698x; cf. Harris, 1978, 1, 190). Arndt & Gingrich state, "The uses of this prep. are so many-sided, and oft., so easily confused, that a strictly systematic treatment is impossible" (1957, 257).

The preposition ἐν helps indicate the relations of objects spatially, temporally, or ideologically. A way out of this complexity is offered by Dana & Mantey (1955, 96-115) who identify a root, resultant, and remote meaning for prepositions. They identify the root meaning of ἐν as "within," resultant meanings as "in, on, at, within, among, with, by means of, and while," and remote meanings as "besides, into, and because of" (105). The decision for any given meaning is determined by several factors relating to authorial usage, context, and apparent spatial, temporal, or ideational emphasis. It is of interest to note that the major commentaries do not even comment upon ἐν as a separate word in John 1:1. It is so connected with ἀρχη, "the beginning," and associations with Genesis 1:1, "In the beginning God created," that its basic meaning in John 1:1 appears undisputed. It appears safe to conclude that ἐν in John 1:1 basically means "in," and connotes a temporal relation to "the beginning."

2. ἀρχη: According to Delling, ἀρχη "always signifies 'primacy,' whether in time," or ". . . rank" (1964, 478). If the context suggests primacy of time, ἀρχη refers to the starting point of the time period indicated. Hence, "beginning," and "origin," are given as the basic meanings of ἀρχη in this sense (cf. Bullinger, 1877, 92; Thayer, 1885, 76; and, Arndt & Gingrich, 1957, 111). If the context suggests primacy of rank, ἀρχη refers to the status of the person exercising influence. Hence, ἀρχη is translated as chief, ruler, leader, dominion, power, etc.

The context of John 1:1 makes the basic meaning of ἀρχη as "beginning" undisputed for the following reasons: (a) the Genesis creation account is clearly alluded to in John 1:1-5. Not only are the ideas of creation similar (e.g., God; the Word of God; the beginning; creation; light; darkness) but several of the actual words of the Greek translation of Genesis are utilized (e.g., ἐν ἀρχη, θεος, ἐγενετο, φως, σκοτια); (b) ἐν ἀρχη exactly reproduces the Greek translation of the Hebrew בראשית (berishith) of Genesis 1:1; ἐν is the common word used for ב (in) throughout the Hebrew Bible; ἀρχη is the common word used for ראשית (beginning); and, (c) the alternative meaning of ἀρχη as "primacy of rank" would be exceedingly forced and strained. Therefore, it seems beyond dispute that the basic meaning of ἀρχη is "beginning" in a temporal sense.

3. ἠν: This is the 3rd person, singular, imperfect, active, indicative form of the Greek verb εἰμι, the verb of being. The present tense of this verb is translated, "he, she, or it is." Hence, the past, or imperfect tense is "he, she, or it was." Essentially, ἠν means "was" (past tense) as opposed to "is" (present tense). Yet, two considerations are important for understanding the grammar of this common verb, namely, its tense and its functions. Admittedly, these considerations move us beyond lexical to grammatical concerns (the stated focus of the next chapter). But a judgment is here made as to the appropriateness of mixing lexical and grammatical concerns for a proper understanding of the basic meaning of ἠν.

In English, the tense of a verb indicates time, past (was), present (is), or future (will be). In Greek, tense indicates not only the time of an action, but, more so, its manner. Dana & Mantey identify three manners in which the action of a Greek verb may be conceived: (a) it is portrayed as continuous; (b) complete; or, (c) as simply occurring, without reference to its ongoingness or completion (1955, 178).

There are several possible grammatical functions for ἦν. A different function is evident for each of its three occurrences in John 1:1: in 1:1a ἦν functions as an "affirmation of existence" (the Word *was*); in 1:1b ἦν functions as a "statement of relationship" (the Word *was* with God); in 1:1c ἦν functions as a "predication" (the Word *was* God). The preceeding paragraph, discussing the matter of tense, is only relevant to 1:1a, "the Word was." The manner of affirmation of existence here is continuous, as opposed to complete, or simply as occurring. These grammatical considerations become critical in Trinitarian and Unitarian debates, as will become evident in subsequent chapters. For now, it is sufficient to note that the basic meaning of ἦν is "was," indicating not only past time, but also continuous existence, at least for the use of ἦν in 1:1a. The other two occurrences indicate different functions. In 1:1b, a relationship is affirmed. In 1:1c a predication is made. At the interpretive level there is considerable debate as to Trinitarian and Unitarian implications. Nevertheless, the basic meaning of ἦν, as the past tense (was) of the verb of being (is) remains undisputed.

4. ὁ: This is the Greek definite article. Its basic meaning in English is "the." But the function of "the" in Greek differs slightly from that in English. Once again, grammatical considerations are necessary. The Greek definite article evolved from the Greek demonstrative pronoun (οὗτος,ἐκεινος/this, that), originally having very strong identity and pointing functions (cf. Robertson, 1934, 754-56). In time, and through usage, the definite article came to be distinguished from the demonstrative, losing some, but not all, of its identity and pointing capacity. Hence, the basic function of the article, as used in NT times, is "to point out individual identity," or to mark an object as "definitely conceived" (Dana & Mantey, 1957, 137). For example, in referring to a house, or a boat, or a soldier, the Greek would draw attention to a specific house (like the White House), a specific boat (like the Titanic), or a specific soldier (like George Washington), by the use of an article. Hence, when referring to **the** house, **the** boat, or **the** soldier, in given contexts, it would be understood that a specific, definite, or well-known object was in mind. The application of this identity and pointing capacity in John 1:1 is obvious and significant.

The definite article is used with God (1:1b), and Word (1:1a, b, and c). These references, then, can be assumed to be specific, well-known, and understood (i.e., **the** God, **the** Word). A helpful distinction, for the reader unfamiliar with the force of the Greek article, may be put this way: the force of "the" in Greek lies somewhere in between the flat English use of "the" and the sharp and pointed English use of "this" (the immediate demonstrative pronoun), or "that" (the remote demonstrative pronoun). Hence, the basic meaning of ὁ is an emphatic **the**, lending specificity and definiteness to its object. The fact that in Greek, unlike in English, there is no indefinite article (i.e., "a"), complicates the interpretation of John 1:1c, θεος ἠν ὁ λογος (note: there is no "the" before θεος in this clause). This matter will be addressed in the next chapter when grammatical considerations will be in full focus.

5. λογος: Of all the words in John 1:1 λογος is by far the most complex. This is due to the significantly rich and diverse usage of λογος in both Greek and Jewish philosophical and religious speculation. As much ink has been spilled over the interpretation of this term as any other in the history of Western culture. Major commentaries often provide a special appendix or excursus to discuss λογος. Entire monographs have labored over the exposition of its meaning (e.g., Lovelady, 1963). An attempt will be made here to arrive at the basic meaning of λογος by summarizing this extensive scholarship.

The noun λογος derives from the verb λεγειν, which basically means, to say. Hence, λογος, the noun, conveys the thing said, or simply put, the word. Originally, λεγειν meant "to gather," to "pick out things which from some standpoint are alike" (Debrunner, 1967, 72). In mathematics it conveyed the sense of "counting," in storytelling the sense of "narrating," or "enumerating," the events of an account. Eventually, λογος came to be understood as the account itself, and then, the reason, or grounds of an account. This etymological background is helpful in understanding how λογος came to prominence in philosophical and religious systems as a symbol for ideas, reason, mind, thought, and even ultimate reality.

The λογος concept features prominently in ancient Babylonian, Egyptian, Greek, Roman, Jewish, and Christian thought (Lovelady, 1963, traces the major developments in each of these traditions). One key to grasping the complexity and richness of its history and development is in noting that the concept developed not only within various traditions, but among and between traditions. The author of the gospel of John seized upon its popularity, exploiting its familiarity, in order to effectively announce the thesis of his gospel. But, just what precise content was intended by his use of λογος remains much debated. In the main, the debate has boiled down to a choice between Greek and Hebrew emphases, the consensus being with the latter (cf. Davies, 1996, 43-64). Some, like Dodd (1968), prefer the synthesis offered by Philo of Alexandria. The differences between Greek and Hebrew emphases are now summarized.

In Greek thought, the λογος was conceived of as an impersonal energy, force, idea, structure, or principle guiding and controlling the universe. It was not conceived of as a person, but as an impersonal abstraction. This understanding is reflected in the philosophies of Heraclitus, Anaxagorus, Plato, Aristotle, and Zeno (cf. Lovelady, 1963, 47-58). In Hebrew thought, however, the λογος concept developed within the "word" (Hebrew: דבר, dabar;

Aramaic: מֵמְרָא, memra) and "wisdom" (Hebrew: הָכְמָא; hokma) traditions. In these traditions word and wisdom were at times personified, bordering on hypostatization (i.e., presenting the λογος as a distinct being). In other words, the λογος concept developed as a way of speaking about the transcendent God in immanent terms. Dunn summarizes the Jewish view this way: "the logos of God is God in his self-revelation" (1980, 230). Although the Jewish λογος in the word and wisdom traditions was often presented as an intermediary being, alongside of God, Jewish monotheism was always maintained. The λογος concept was simply a metaphor for the "immanence" of God. This understanding is clearly evident in Philo's synthesis of Jewish and Greek emphases (cf. Dodd, 1968, 54-73; and, Dunn, 1980, 241-44).

But, John's prologue presents a problem for previous understandings of the λογος, whether as an abstract principle of order in the universe, or as a personification, a metaphor for God's revelatory activity. The problematic innovation of John's gospel is found in the assertion that this λογος "became flesh" (John 1:14). The critical issue is the way in which the λογος is to be identified with the human person, Jesus Christ. How could Jesus, an actual, distinct, and historical individual, be identified with, or as, the λογος of God, without comprimising Jewish monotheism, or yielding to pagan polytheism? The Trinity is the traditional answer. Unitarians, however, soften, in various ways, the identification of Jesus with, or as, the λογος.

The basic meaning of λογος in John 1:1 is not very basic. Its meaning is complicated by several considerations: (a) the profundity of the λογος concept; (b) the popularity of the λογος concept; (c) the long intricate development of this concept both within and among traditions; (d) its potential to be understood as an abstraction; (e) its potential to be understood as a metaphor for God's revelatory activity; (f) its potential to be understood in terms of an hypostasis, an intermediary being; and, perhaps most telling for the focus of this commentary, (g) the way in which λογος is related to the man, Jesus Christ. It is hoped that the basic meaning of the λογος in John 1:1 will receive greater clarity as we progress through the upcoming steps of interpretation.

6. και: This is a conjunction with several possible meanings. A conjunction connects words, phrases, clauses, and sentences in various relations. As a conjunction, και may be: (a) transitional, or continuative, meaning, "and"; (b) adjunctive, meaning, "also"; (c) ascensive, meaning, "even"; (d) adversative, meaning, "but"; or, (e) emphatic, meaning, "indeed" (cf. Dana & Mantey, 1957, 249-52). Context determines usage. Only meaning (a) makes sense in John 1:1. Και is used 15 x in the prologue of John. In each occurrence, except in John 1:16 where meaning (c) is preferred, the obvious meaning is "and." John's prologue is often noted for its poetic features (cf. Brown, 1966, 18). These are served by this understanding of και. The plain meaning of και as "and" serves the intricate staircase parallelism of the prologue, help-

ing the reader to witness transitions in the career of the λογος, from pre-existence (John 1:1, 2), to creation (1:3-5), to revelation (1:9-13), to incarnation (1:14), to ascension (1:18). I am unaware of any commentator suggesting any other meaning for και in these occurrences.

7. προς: The shade of meaning of Greek prepositions varies with the case of the noun with which they are used. In John 1:1 προς is used with θεον, a noun in the accusative case. Lexicographers collectively identify the root accusative meaning of προς as near, or towards, in the sense of facing (cf. Dana & Mantey, 1957, 110; Bullinger, 1877, 888; Thayer, 1885, 541; Arndt & Gingrich, 1957, 716; Reicke, 1968, 721; Robertson, 1934, 625; and, Harris, 1978, 1, 204). John's choice of προς is significant when compared with his options. Several Greek prepositions (εν, μετα, παρα, εις, περι, επι, συν) may convey the sense of something or someone being "with" something or someone else, but of these only προς is best suited to emphasize "personal intercourse rather than simply spatial juxtaposition or personal accompaniment" (Harris, 1978, 1, 205; cf. also: Bullinger, 1877, 888; Bultmann, 1971, 32; Brown, 1966, 5; and, Schnackenburg, 1968, 234). Hence, προς lends support to the view that the λογος is understood by John as a personal being, distinct from God, but in the beginning as "God" in some sense. Unitarians who would argue for an impersonal understanding of λογος in John 1:1b (e.g., Wierwille, 1975, 81-90) do so awkwardly, either neglecting to comment upon the significance of προς, or failing to apprehend its implications. Trinitarian and Unitarian debates swirl around the implications of several details in John 1:1, the significance of προς proving no exception. Although the interpretive implications of this preposition may generate controversy, its basic meaning as "with," in the sense of "near, towards, or facing," stands firm!

8. θεος: Bullinger (1877, 331) provides a lengthy, interesting, and helpful introduction to the basic meaning of this commonplace, but sacred, term.

A name reclaimed from the heathen, and used in N. T. for the true God. Various derivations, ancient, and modern, have been proposed, but it is nearly certain that its origin is from the East and comes from the Sanscrit root, DIU-S. . . which means (1) masc., fire, the sun, (2) fem., a ray of light, day* (hence Lat, Dies [fem] day), (3) neut., the sky, heaven. DIV-S also means (1) as adj., brilliant, (2) as fem. subst. sky or heaven. Whenever the Sun shines in the world he has been or is, worshipped as god, because he gives light to Heaven and life to earth; and heaven was in turn worshipped as the abode of the sun, but the object of adoration was Light and Life, or heaven either as the abode of the sun, or as personified. Then DIAUS was procreating or generating power dwelling in heaven. The Father of Light and Life. Hence came the Lat. DEUS . . .

θεος however, having lost the meaning of the one God came to
mean "a god" only, one of many gods. Hence it became necessary
in N. T. gen., to distinguish it by the article, ὁ θεος.

A wide range of meanings came to be associated with θεος in both its
Jewish and pagan uses. It conveyed: (a) the supreme reality of the universe;
conceived personally (Jewish and pagan) or impersonally (pagan); (b) the
one true God of Israel; (c) the deities of pagan polytheism (e.g., Zeus, Apollo);
and, (d) angels, intermediary beings, kings, heroes, or great leaders in both
Jewish and pagan sources (clear examples are found in Cartlidge & Dungan,
1980, 13-22).

The gospel of John uses θεος 93x. In all of these occurrences the reference is *clearly* to the one true God of Israel, except in John 1:1c, and 10: 34-
35. John 10:34-35 reads as follows: "Jesus answered them, 'Is it not written
in your law, I said Ye are gods?' If he called them gods, unto whom the word
of God came. . . " (King James Version). The reference here is to Psalm 82:6,
where men, inept leaders of the Jewish nation, are called "gods." This is an
example of (d) above. This reference is important in Trinitarian and Unitarian
debates as the context of this quote involves a justification of Jesus' claim to
be one with the Father (10:30), a man making himself God (10:33). Brown
suggests that Jesus' quotation of Psalm 82 reflects an a *fortiori* argument.
That is to say, "if it is permissible to call men gods because they were ve-
hicles of the Word of God, how much more permissible is it to use 'God' of
him who *is* (italics original) the Word of God" (1966, 410). Further reflection
or comment at this time would necessitate changing the title of this commentary to JOHN 10:30-33 AS PROOFTEXT, and require a rewrite of all that has
preceded.

John 1:1c does contain a use of θεος that *may* be understood in some
sense other than the basic meaning θεος consistently has throughout John's
gospel. A decision, however, awaits the refinement of subsequent steps of
interpretation. For now, θεος in John 1:1b follows usage (b) above, the precise understanding of the usage in 1:1c awaits further refinement.

[1] ἐν
[2] ἀρχη
[3] ἦν
[4] ὁ
[5] λογος
[6] και
[7] προς
[8] θεος

Chapter Three

John 1:1 and Grammatical Criticism

This chapter will explore the grammatical aspects of John 1:1. Initially, each word will be grammatically described. The focus will then shift to the relationships between words, phrases, and clauses. As we proceed these grammatical relations will be diagrammed. At critical points issues relevant to Trinitarian and Unitarian understandings will be raised. The chapter concludes with a full diagram, illustrating the grammatical relationships of all of John 1:1.

As noted in the previous chapter there are 17 words in John 1:1. A grammatical description of each of these words is now provided as a foundation for further discussion. These descriptions are based on *The analytical Greek lexicon* (1975; published by Zondervan).

1:1a
> ἐν· a preposition; properly referring to place, here meaning "in" (137).
> ἀρχῇ·: noun; the dative singular of ἀρχη (54).
> ἦν: verb; the third person singular imperfect of εἰμι (187).
> ὁ: the nominative masculine singular article (281).
> λογος: noun; the nominative singular subject (253).

1:1b
> καὶ: conjunction; here meaning "and" (208).
> ὁ: the nominative singular article (281).
> λογος: noun; the nominative singular subject (253).
> ἦν: verb; the third person singular imperfect of εἰμι (187).
> προς: preposition; here meaning "with" (346).

15

τον: the accusative singular article (281).
θεον: noun; the accusative singular of θεος (192).

1:1c

καὶ: conjunction; here meaning "and" (208).
θεος: noun; the predicate nominative (193).
ἦν: verb; the third person singular imperfect of εἰμι (187).
ὁ: the nominative singular article (281).
λογος: noun; the nominative singular subject (253).

In order to grasp the relationships between words and phrases it is necessary to begin with the larger grammatical unit, the clause. The relationships between and among the three clauses of John 1:1 can then be appreciated at the conclusion of our study.

In the first clause of John 1:1 the subject is λογος, made definite by the article ὁ. Hence, the subject is ὁ λογος, a reference apparently well known or understood by John's readers. The article functions somewhat like an adjective, describing the Word. This relation may be diagrammed thus:

$$\frac{\lambda o \gamma o \varsigma}{|\dot{o}}$$

The verb here is ἦν, understood as an affirmation of the continuous existence of ὁ λογος. This relation may be diagrammed thus:

$$\frac{\lambda o \gamma o \varsigma \ |\dot{\eta} \nu}{|\dot{o}}$$

ἐν ἀρχη is an adverbial prepositional phrase, modifying the verb ἦν, answering the question, When was the Word? This relation may be diagrammed thus:

$$\frac{\lambda o \gamma o \varsigma \ |\dot{\eta}\nu}{|\dot{o} \quad |\dot{\epsilon}\nu \ \dot{\alpha}\rho\chi\eta}$$

Many confidently conclude that the **eternity** of the Word is here affirmed (e.g., Barth, 1968, 21; Boismard, 1957, 7; Robertson, 1932, 3; Brown, 1966, 4; Bultmann, 1971, 31; Lindars, 1972, 82; and, Schnackenburg, 1968, 232). The logic of their position is as follows: if only God is eternal, and the Word is eternal, then clearly, the Word is God. This, perhaps, is what John 1:1c echoes (θεος ἦν ὁ λογος/ the Word was God). Trinitarians seize upon these perceptions. But, Unitarians exercise caution at this point. The next paragraph explains why.

If John 1:1a ("in the beginning") alludes to Genesis 1:1 ("in the beginning"), then a consideration of the interpretation of this phrase in Genesis is relevant. Simply put: Does the phrase "in the beginning" refer to an absolute starting point, or does it refer to some relative point in time? If absolute, Trinitarian logic with regard to the eternality of the Word is supported. If relative, then the door remains open to qualifying or mitigating the divinity of the Word in some way.

A case is made for the absolute interpretation in the following manner: (a) John 1:1c does affirm that the Word was God, a possible echo of 1:1a; (b) John 1:3, in presenting ὁ λογος as the agent of creation, does so in a way that expressly underlines the absoluteness of 1:1a ("all things were made by him; and without him was not any thing made that was made," King James Version). Included in the "not any thing" of John 1:3 would be both space and time. Hence, the absolute eternality and transcendence of the Word. Furthermore, the contrast between the ἠν (was; 1:1) of the λογος and the ἐγενετο (became; 1:3) of creation seems intended (this point is argued by Pollard, 1958, 148); and, (c) other passages in John may be understood as supporting this view (e.g., John 8:58, "Before Abraham was, I am"; and 17:5, "And now, O Father, glorify thou me... with the glory which I had with thee before the world was"; both King James Version).

A case for the relative interpretation is made in the following manner: (a) the λογος in John's prologue contains several parallels to the wisdom traditions in Judaism (e.g., being with God in the beginning; being the instrument of creation; being the instrument of revelation; experiencing rejection; "dwelling" in Israel, or among the people of God; these parallels are generously illustrated by Boring, Berger, & Colpe, 1995, 238). In this tradition wisdom is spoken of as being "created" before the foundation of the world (Proverbs 8:22-24). Hence, the parallels suggest that the λογος is a created being too! The logic here is as follows: the λογος concept in John is constructed upon the analogy of Jewish wisdom traditions. Wisdom is said to have been created. Hence, the λογος is created. If created, the λογος cannot be eternal, and therefore is not God, at least not as the Father is God. This was precisely the argument of Arius, the most famous Unitarian of church history. Arius' famous slogan, "there was a time when the Son was not" (taken from Arius' letter to Eusebius as found in Rusch, 1980, 30), is to the point; (b) in addition to the notion that wisdom was created, several other realities were understood as being created *prior* to "the beginning." Most noted among these are: Torah; the Throne of Glory; the Patriarchs; the nation of Israel; the Sanctuary; and the name of the Messiah. Technically, only the first two in this list were "created," the others were said to be "comprehended" in the mind of God (cf. Dodd, 1968, 85). If, in Jewish thought, several realities existed prior to "the beginning," the case for the eternality of the λογος, and his subsequent deity, are called into question; and, (c) passages which suggest the superiority of the Father to the Son, or the dependency of the Son on the Father, may be interpreted in light of the suggestion that the λογος was created. John 14:28, "My Father is greater than I," and, 16:28, "I came forth from the Father," and, 5:19, "I say unto you, The Son can do nothing of himself," all come to mind (Jesus being the "I" in these passages).

This lengthy reflection on the grammatical implications of John 1:1a more properly belongs to the subsequent steps of source and/or composition criticism. But a decision to enter this reflection now demonstrates both the simultaniety of interpretive steps and the fact that interpretation is an art. After all, it was *my* decision to state these reflections at this time! No doubt they are critical to an eventual Trinitarian or Unitarian verdict. A verdict that must await the refinement of further steps. Patience is no stranger to scholarship!

The relationship between 1:1a and 1:1b is provided by και, understood here in its continuative sense as "and." Clauses may be related to each other in a coordinate or in a subordinate manner (cf. Dana & Mantey, 1957, 269). The understanding of και as "and" establishes the clausal relationship as coordinate. Clause 1:1b picks up where 1:1a left off, providing additional and coordinate information. This relationship will be illustrated in the diagram at the end of the discussion of 1:1b.

Again, the subject of the second clause is λογος, modified by the article ὁ. The verb again is ἦν, only here, not affirming existence, but stating a relationship. This relationship is modified by the adverbial prepositional phrase προς τον θεον, answering the question, Who was the Word in relation to? God (θεον in the accusative case) is indicated as the one true God by means of the definite article. These relationships, and those of the first clause of John 1:1, are now illustrated:

The relationship between clauses 1:1b and 1:1c is provided for by και, understood in its continuative sense. The independent, yet coordinate, relationships between **all** the clauses of John 1:1 will be illustrated at the end of the discussion of this third and final clause.

The subject of 1:1c is clearly ὁ λογος, indicated as such by the article. In clauses containing both a subject noun and a predicate noun the former is distinguished from the latter by the presence of the article (cf. Blass, Debrunner,

& Funk, 1961, 143). In 1:1c, then, ὁ λογος is subject, θεος is predicate. The verb again is ἠν, here serving the predication. The relationships of this clause may be diagrammed thus:

λογος | ἠν | θεος
| ὁ

The understanding of the grammatical implications of the predicate θεος is, perhaps, the most hotly contested matter in Trinitarian and Unitarian debates. The following issues need to be considered: (1) the choice of the noun θεος rather than the adjective θειος; (2) the possible definiteness, indefiniteness, or qualitative understanding of the predicate θεος; and, (3) relevant contextual considerations.

(1): Trinitarians argue that if John wanted to clearly downplay a possible equation between the Being of God and that of the Word he could have utilized the word θειος. Bullinger defines this term as "pertaining to θεος, what is God's, or proceeds from him, divine" (1887, 335). Bromiley identifies θειος as an adjective of θεος, explaining its appropriateness to "seers, priests, singers, saviors, and rulers" (1985, 331). Essentially, the term means "godlike," but stops short of suggesting a full equality with God. Had John chosen this term later interpreters may have been spared the Trinitarian/Unitarian debate. The λογος would clearly have been understood as "divine," but not necessarily as God, or equal to God in any full or absolute sense. Yet, the choice of θεος rather than θειος does not automatically force one into a Trinitarian corner. A great deal of debate revolves around the fact that θεος in John 1:1c is anarthrous, that is, it is not preceeded by ὁ.

(2): When a noun is anarthrous, Greek grammar allows for three possibilities: (a) it is understood to be definite, even without an article; (b) it is understood to be indefinite, suggesting that the reference is "a" something or other, one of many; or, (c) it is understood in a qualitative sense, suggesting that the reference participates in the nature of the noun used. Each of these possibilities need to be explored and explained.

(a): This commentary has already discussed the function of the definite article, noting its origin from the demonstrative pronoun and its identity and pointing capacity (see pages 26-27). In Greek, the use of the article with θεος, or any other given noun, makes it clear that THE God, or THE whatever, is indicated. Yet, Greek grammar allows for this same definiteness, even without an article. Such is the case in instances when the noun is so well known, or so common, as to not need an article, or could be discerned from context as already definite (cf. Dana & Mantey, 1957, 149). A clear example is at hand. In John 1:1a the word "ἀρχη" is without the article, but by context and allusion to Genesis 1:1, is clearly understood as definite, a reference to THE beginning. But the definiteness of θεος in 1:1c seems excluded, at least in the sense of identity and interchangeability with the λογος. This is made clear by the distinction pressed in 1:1b, where it is stated that "the Word was with God (ὁ λογος ἠν προς τον θεον)." Hence, other grammatical possibilities need to be explored.

(b): One possibility is to treat the anarthrous use of θεος as indefinite, supplying the word "a" before it. Hence, the thought would be that the Word was "a god," one among many (perhaps, due to the Jewish background, angels might be appropriate, see Collins, 1997, 82-88). Several objections, however, come to mind:

(i) John 1:1c θεος ἠν ὁ λογος seems to parallel 1:14 ὁ λογος σαρξ εγενετο (the Word became flesh). Would John have us translate, the Word became "a flesh"? (note: σαρξ/flesh is anarthrous like θεος/God)

(ii) Another telling example of the definiteness of a Greek noun without an article is provided by John 8:54: ". . . it is my Father that honoreth me; of whom ye say, that he is your **God/** ἐστιν ὁ πατηρ μου ὁ δοξαζων με ὁν ὑμεις λεγετε ὁτι **θεος** ἡμων ἐστιν." I have put God/θεος in bold type to draw the reader's attention to the fact that the noun, although anarthrous, is definite. The reference in context is clear enough that THE God is intended. No one would recommend the translation "a god" in this instance!

(iii) Word order in Greek grammar suggests that predicate nouns are distinguished from subject nouns, not only by the absence of the article, but also by word order. In many instances this is made clear by an anarthrous predicate preceeding the verb, as is the case in John 1:1c (θεος **ἠν** ὁ λογος). Scholarly treatments of this phenomenon giving significant attention to John 1:1 are provided by Colwell (1933) and Harner (1973).

(iv) If John 1:1 provides the thesis statement of the gospel, which is likely, due to the fact that it is both the first verse and is so majestic, then the body of the gospel should cohere. In other words, Is Jesus presented in John's gospel as God, or as a god? Two sets of two verses each, in my judgment, argue that John's gospel presents Jesus as God.

The first set of two verses are 1:18 and 20:28. These are significant verses for the question under consideration for two reasons: (a) both verses form an inclusion with 1:1; and, (b) both verses use the term θεος as a title for Jesus. An inclusion is a figure of speech where a word or concept, mentioned at the beginning of a unit of thought, is repeated at the end of that unit (cf. Bullinger, 1887, 245). The prologue begins by calling Jesus God (1:1c) and ends by attributing to him the title "unique God" (μονογενης θεος). The gospel begins by calling Jesus God (1:1c) and ends (approximately; or climatically) with the confession of Thomas, "My Lord and my God" (ὁ κυριος μου και ὁ θεος μου). Note that the definite article is used with θεος in this instance. Although the title θεος is not used of Jesus *frequently* in John's gospel, it certainly is used *strategically*.

The second set of two verses are 5:18 and 10:33. These are significant verses for two reasons: (a) both verses are polemically oriented; and, (b) both verses relate the term θεος to Jesus. John 5:18 states: "Therefore the Jews sought the more to kill him, because he not only had broken the sabbath, but said also that God was his Father, making himself equal to God." The Greek text of the last three words is as follows: "ισον . . . τω θεω". Clearly, THE God is intended. Context makes it clear that Jesus is claiming the exclusive prerogatives of God, namely, power to give and to take life. John 10:33 states: "The Jews answered him, saying, 'For a good work we stone thee not; but for blasphemy; and because that thou being a man, makest thyself God' ." The Greek text of the last three words here is as follows: "ποιεις σεαυτον θεος". Although an article is absent from θεος, context argues for the definiteness of the reference. It does not seem from either of these contexts that Jesus is being persecuted for claiming to be "a god." Something more seems to have provoked the response of a possible stoning. Supportive of this contextual reasoning is an episode in John 8 where Jesus claims, "Before Abraham was, I am" (8:58). The response here was an attempt to stone Jesus. The episode of 10:33 explicitly makes reference to this previous episode (see especially 10:31), thus linking the two episodes.

A verdict for John 1:1 as a prooftext for Trinitarianism, however, is far from secure, as a final consideration under this point will make clear.

(v) While many scholars will allow that θεος in John 1:1c is definite in some sense, their understanding of this definiteness falls short of the traditional Trinitarian confession that "Jesus is true God of true God." The subtle qualification made here is between a functional versus an ontological understanding of the affirmation that Jesus is God. To say that Jesus is God functionally is to say that Jesus, as the λογος, represents God, but is not in himself (ontologically) God. To say that Jesus is God ontologically is to say that Jesus represents God because he in fact is God. Admittedly, it is difficult to find support in John's gospel for a distinction that, perhaps, he never intended. Another slight, but hopefully helpful, digression on this point may prevent the reader undue despair.

In the Ancient Near East when somebody was sent to represent someone else, usually a servant representing his master, or a merchant, or a king, or a nobleman of some kind, they were invested with the authority of the one who had sent them. This would be similar to our culture's understanding of "power of attorney." But first century Judaism went beyond present day understandings of representation. The person sent not only acted on behalf of the sender, but could be addressed and honored as if he were really that person! Regarding this phenomenon Greene states, "The role and purpose of the messenger, then, was primarily that of extending temporally and geographically the existing power of one person's spoken words or will; allowing that person to be in two places at once" (1989, 7). In other words, God could maintain his transcendent status in heaven while at the same time be present (in Jesus) on earth. But, as you might discern, the understanding of the sender and the sendee's identity was functional, not ontological. This concept in Judaism is known as the shaliach (שליח; cf. Steinsaltz, 1989, 266). Some scholars would advocate that Jesus be understood along the lines of the Jewish shaliach, one who represented God functionally, and hence could be given the title of God, but not one who was ontologically God. Hence, the constraints of Jewish monotheism are not compromised to their way of thinking (this is the approach of Harvey, 1982).

(c): Having ruled out "definiteness" (THE God), and "indefiniteness" (a god), a third grammatical possibility remains. θεος is simply a qualitative predicate, laying emphasis upon the intrinsic nature of the Word. Trinitarians would insist that John 1:1a affirms the eternality of the Word, 1:1b distinguishes the person of the Word from that of the Father (God), and 1:1c predicates the equality of the Word with the nature of the Father (God). In other words, the Word is not identical with the Father as a person(ὁ θεος), but is equal to the Father in nature (θεος). This *possible* qualitative understanding of the predicate in Greek grammar is documented by Harner (1973). Its *probability* depends on one's verdicts with regard to several issues which, as of yet, appear unresolved.

(3): Several relevant contextual considerations have already been considered under the discussions of (a), (b), and (c) above. This final segment of the chapter will entertain just a few more.

The chief contributor to the grammatical dilemmas of John 1:1 is the apparent paradox of 1:1b and 1:1c, the propositions that "the Word was with God," and, that "the Word was God." The major difficulty has been deciding on the definiteness, indefiniteness, or qualitativeness of θεος in 1:1c. Although definiteness, in the sense of the interchangeable identities of the λογος and the θεος, seems ruled out, due to the paradox of 1:1b and 1:1c, other pertinent information from the immediate context needs to be considered. John 1:2, "the same was in the beginning with God," appears to repeat the essential information of 1:1a and 1:1b. Three observations are relevant here: (a) the reiteration of 1:1a and 1:1b in 1:2 strengthens the sense of the unity of 1:1; (b) 1:1, as a unity, appears to have a staircase parallelism; and, (c) the use of θεος in 1:2 seems to militate against the proposal of any "unannounced" differing sense in 1:1c, hence, suggesting some kind of definiteness. Since point (a) is obvious, only points (b) and (c) demand additional comment.

(b): The apparent "staircase parallelism" of John 1:1 is understood as follows: John 1:1 is comprised of three clauses, each asserting something about the λογος. In a "staircase parallelism" each successive clause builds on the previous, the climax occurring in the third clause. This way of understanding John 1:1 suggests that 1:1b says something more profound than does 1:1a, and that 1:1c says something more profound than does 1:1b. "In the beginning was the Word" (an affirmation of pre-existence), "and the Word was with God" (a statement of relationship in the realm of pre-existence), "and the Word was God" (a statement regarding the intrinsic identity of the Word). It seems to me that the translation of 1:1c, "the Word was a god," must be excluded, if John is to be understood along these lines. This thought would be anti-climatic to the previous clause, suggesting that the Word was less than the God with whom He was with.

(c): John uses θεος/God 3x in the first two verses of his gospel, 1:1b, 1:1c, and 1:2. Three arguments may be given to suggest that in each case the reference is to the same reality, although with a slight, but not insignificant, qualification. (i) It would be extremely awkward for an author to introduce a reference so common as "God," with varying meanings, without some sort of "advanced" warning, or a clear indication of a variant usage; (ii) The poetry of the prologue, if it is to be consistent, demands a uniform sense to θεος/God in 1:1b, 1:1c, and 1:2. Throughout the prologue the author has shifted his movement of thought by means of catch-words, in every instance employing the same meaning for each word (e.g.: λογος/Word in 1:1a and 1:1b; θεος/God in 1:1b and 1:1c; αυτου εγενετο/through him became in 1:3; ζωη/life in 1:4; φως/light in 1:7, 1:8, and, 1:9; and, κοσμος/world in 1:9 and 1:10). The burden of explanation lies with those who suggest an equivocal meaning for θεος/God in 1:b, 1:1c, and 1:2; and, (iii) The author does, later, introduce some grounds upon which the apparent paradox of 1:1b and 1:1c can be reconciled. In 1:18, the author makes it clear that "the God" in view in 1:1b was "the Father." This he does by explicitly referring to the companion of the λογος as "the Father/του πατρος," at the end of the prologue. This perception is reinforced by the apparent design of the prologue and the inclusive nature of 1:1 and 1:18. The prologue begins with an affirmation of the Word's pre-existence, relationship to God, and intrinsic nature (1:1). The prologue proceeds with comments about the Word's role in creation (1:3-5), revelation (1:10-12), incarnation (1:14), and redemption (1:17), concluding with affirmations regarding the Word's post-existence, relationship with the Father, and intrinsic nature (1:18).

In conclusion, the troublesome anarthrous θεος of 1:1c is best understood in its definite sense, a reference to THE God, but not in terms of particular identity, since the author of John has qualified this by indicating a distinction between the Father and the Son. One is left with a qualitative understanding, suggesting that the Father and the Son share the same divine nature. This conclusion points in a Trinitarian direction. Yet, the issue of the eternality of the Word, and the debate over a functional versus an ontological understanding of the role of the λογος, need further consideration. For now, it remains to offer a complete diagram of the grammatical relations of John 1:1.

λογος |ἦν
‾‾|ὁ‾‾‾‾‾‾‾|‾ ἐν ἀρχη

και

λογος |ἦν
‾‾|ὁ‾‾‾‾‾‾‾|‾ προς τον θεον

και

λογος |ἦν |θεος
‾‾|ὁ‾‾

Chapter Four

John 1:1 and Translation Criticism

This chapter will analyze 15 translations of John 1:1 representing the decisions of 25 different committees and/or individuals. These translations present both major and minor renditions of John 1:1 in English publications from 1582 to 1986. An explanation of translation procedures and theories preceeds an analysis of these translations. The reader can anticipate learning something about the problems of translation as well as the bases for making translation decisions. A competent translation of John 1:1 presupposes the considerations of textual, lexical, and grammatical criticism (Chapters 1, 2, and 3). In addition, the competence of any given translation needs to be evaluated in light of interpretive decisions based on many of the other methods mentioned in the Introduction (e.g., rhetorical; form; source; redaction; and, composition criticism; see pages xiv-xv). Although this text is limited to the explicit discussions of textual, lexical, grammatical, and translation criticism (Chapters 1-4) many of the other methods have been indirectly or implicitly considered. The interpretive problems, options, and insights discussed in the previous chapters are reflected in these 15 translations. Hence, this chapter provides a review of essential points and, hopefully, advances the reader to a position where a Trinitarian or a Unitarian verdict might be given with greater confidence.

To translate is to interpret. This assertion needs to be acknowleged by any translator. Since no two languages are identical, the conversion of one word in one language into that of another requires an interpretive decision. The question then, is, How should one interpret? Translators find themselves on the horns of a dilemma. One horn of this dilemma is finding a word or phrase that is *faithful* to the form of the word or phrase in the original language. The other is finding a word or phrase that is *meaningful* to the audience for which the translator is translating. For example, How should one translate λογος ? A faithful rendition would be Logos, preserving the technical form of the original. A *meaningful* rendition for contemporary English readers would be "Word." A convenient compromise does not seem available. However, in many instances translators find ways to "error" in either direction. This has given rise to four classic translation styles.

These four styles exist on a continuum ranging from *faithfulness to the ancient form* to *contemporary meaningfulness*. The first of these four styles usually takes the form of an **interlinear**, where the original Greek is presented on one line and the corresponding English equivalents are given right underneath the Greek text. Here is an example of this style for John 1:1.

ἐν αρχη ἦν ὁ λογος,   και ὁ λογος ἦν προς τον θεον, και
θεος ἦν   ὁ λογος

in beginning was the Word,   and the Word was with the God, and
God was   the Word

Below each Greek word is the corresponding English word. Usually, in this style of translation, a basic English equivalent is chosen, without frills, bells, or whistles. Having the Greek text right above the English text gives the impression that one is trying to be faithful to the ancient form. Remove the Greek text and one detects a very cumbersome English rendition. Word order is awkward and, in places, the "the" seems to present where it should be absent, and absent where it should be present. This translation style is useful for readers with an intermediate understanding of Greek and a familiarity with reference tools which can lead them to a more precise understanding of certain words or phrases.

The second of the four styles may be referred to as **formal equivalence.** In this style the Greek text is not shown, but an effort is made to maximize faithfulness to the Greek form. Hence, it is a conservative style, rendering Greek into English as closely and consistently as possible, word for word, idiom for idiom, grammatical nuance for grammatical nuance. Few liberties are taken to "spice" up the text with the flavor of contemporary English. Nevertheless, one formal equivalent translation has become a classic of the Modern age. The King James Version of 1611 enjoyed great popularity up to and beyond its anticipated replacements by the English Revised Version (1881), American Revised Version (1941), Revised Standard Version (1952), New International Version (1973), and others. As of 1979 the King James Version has been replaced by the New King James Version. This version has simply replaced some of the archaic expressions, the "thees" and "thous," but preserved its original beauty and formal equivalence. One feature of the King James Version which demonstrates its attempt to be faithful to the original text is its use of *italics*. Italicized words in the King James Version indicate that there is no corresponding Greek word. The translators are letting the reader know that in some instances they had to "*invent*" or "*create*" a word in order to make the translation more meaningful for the English reader. Of the 15 translations we will examine, 9 of them have adopted this translation style.

The third translation style may be referred to as **dynamic equivalence.** In this style an effort is made to maximize meaningfulness to contemporary readers. Hence, it is liberal in efforts to "spice" up the text with contemporary idiom. In this style the form, structure, and grammar of the original is subordinate to the concerns of contemporary relevance. Translators are "freer" to embellish, not for purposes of distortion, but for clarity. Dynamic equivalent translations read with zest and often have an immediate and popular appeal. The common reader often feels "at home" with this type of translation. It is often preferred over the "staid and stuffy" style of some formal equivalent translations. It is sometimes difficult to judge a translation as dynamic rather than as formal since portions of a translation may incorporate both styles. Of the 15 translations to be analyzed, only 2 are clearly and consistently identified as demonstrating this style.

The fourth translation style is **paraphrase**. In this style a radical departure is taken from the structures of the original form. An effort is made not only to be meaningful and relevant but also to clarify the sense of the original in its full context. Hence, words and phrases which often have no support from the original Greek are introduced into this type of translation. The translators are not attempting to "create" a new meaning, but to convey what they believe to be the "contextual sense" of the original in a new context for contemporary readers. Paraphrases often "entertain" their readers with unusually penetrating and precise renditions of the original. One only hopes that these appealing translations are based on sound exegetical and contextual decisions. Of the 15 translations to be analyzed 4 of these are paraphrases. It should come as no surprise to the reader that the paraphrases are either explicitly Trinitarian or explicitly Unitarian. Paraphrases tend to overinterpret in order to remove ambiguities and difficulties for the contemporary reader. Paraphrases most often are products of individuals rather than committees.

The 15 translations will now be presented. The translations are numbered (1-15) and underlined. Below each translation the reader is informed of the style, implications for a Trinitarian and/or Unitarian emphasis, and the individual or versions supporting the translation.

1. In the beginning was the Word, and the Word was with God, and the Word was God.

This is a formal equivalent translation. It is ambiguous on the Trinitarian-

Unitarian controversy. It is supported by the translations of Roman Catholic and mainstream Protestant denominations. (1582: Rheims Version; 1611 Authorized Version; 1881 English Revised Version; 1901 American Revised Version; 1941 Confraternity of Christian Doctrine; 1952 Revised Standard Version; 1973 New International Version; 1985 New Jerusalem Bible; 1986 New American Bible).

2. In the beginning was the Word, and the Word was with God, and the Word was a god.

This is also a formal equivalent translation. It is decidedly Unitarian. It is supported by two individual translators and the Watchtower Bible and Tract Society, the publishing house for the Jehovah's Witnessess. (1808 Archbishop Necome; 1884 The Emphatic Diaglott by Benjamin Wilson; 1950 The New World Translation).

3. Originally was the Word, and the Word was with God, and the Word was God.

This is a formal equivalent translation. It differs from #1 (above) only in replacing "in the beginning" with "originally." It is the product of an individual. (1897 Rotherham's Emphasized Bible).

4. At the beginning the Word already was. The Word was with God, and the Word was God.

This is a formal equivalent translation for 1:1b and 1:1c. 1:1a is a dynamic equivalent translation. It differs from #1 (above) only by replacing "in" with "at" and the addition of the word "already." It is supported by the committee of the 20th Century New Testament. (1901 20th Century New Testament).

5. In the beginning the Word existed. The Word was with God, and the Word was divine.

This is a formal equivalent translation. It is decidedly Unitarian. It is the work of an individual. (1923 Edgar J. Goodspeed).

6. In the beginning was the Word, and the Word was face to face with God, and the Word was God.

This is a formal equivalent translation. It favors a Trinitarian interpretation by emphasizing the personality of the Word in 1:1b. It is the work of an individual. (1924 Montgomery's Centenary Translation).

7. The Logos existed in the very beginning, the Logos was with God, the Logos was divine.

This is a formal equivalent translation. It preserves the technical term

"Logos," but softens the assertion of Deity in 1:1c with the use of "divine" rather than "God." Hence, it favors a Unitarian understanding. It is the work of an individual. (1934 Moffatt's New Translation of the Bible).

8. <u>From the first the Word was in being, and the Word was with God, and the Word was God.</u>
    This is a formal equivalent translation of 1:1b and 1:1c. 1:1a is a dynamic equivalent. It is ambiguous as to a Trinitarian-Unitarian understanding. It is the work of a committee. (1941 Basic English New Testament).

9. <u>In the beginning the Word existed, and the Word was face to face with God, yea, the Word was God Himself.</u>
    This is a dynamic equivalent translation bordering upon a paraphrase. It is decidedly Trinitarian in its emphasis. It is the work of an individual. (1950 Charles B. Williams).

10. <u>In the beginning the Word was existing. And the Word was in fellowship with the Father. And the Word was as to essence absolute Deity.</u>
    This is a paraphrase. It is decidedly Trinitarian. It is the work of an individual. (1956 Kenneth Wuest).

11. <u>At the beginning God expressed Himself. That personal expression, that Word, was with God and was God.</u>
    This is a dynamic equivalent translation. It is ambiguous on the Trinitarian-Unitarian issue. It is the work of an individual. (1958 J. B. Phillips).

12. <u>When all things began, the Word already was. The Word dwelt with God, and what God was the Word was.</u>
    This is a paraphrase. It is more favorable to a Trinitarian understanding. It is the work of a committee. (1961 New English Bible).

13. <u>At the initiation of the time when the creation of the world took place, the Logos-the pre-existent, pre-incarnate Son of God, Who personally intervened in the kosmos for the purpose of creation, preservation, and revelation-This Logos was already existing eternally, and this Personal Logos was experiencing a face to face fellowship with God the Father, and this same Word was the essence of God in the most absolute sense.</u>
    Clearly, this is a paraphrase. It is bending over backwards in order to make the Trinitarian implications of this verse clear. It is the work of an individual. (1963 Edgar J. Lovelady).

14. <u>In the beginning was the Word, and the Word was in God's presence, and the Word was God.</u>

This is a formal equivalent translation. It is ambiguous on the Trinitarian-Unitarian issue. It is the work of an individual. (1966 Raymond E. Brown).

15. In the beginning (before the creation of the world) God was the Word, and the revealed Word was in God's foreknowledge (which was later communicated to man in spoken Words, written Words and the incarnate Word).

This is a paraphrase. It is decidedly Unitarian. Note the attempt to differentiate the Word that was God from the revealed Word in God's foreknowledge. It is the work of an individual. (1975 Victor Paul Wierwille).

These translations can now be reviewed in light of the major interpretive problems raised in Chapters 1-3. For convenience these problems will be identified under four categories: (1) those relating to the verse (John 1:1) as a whole; (2) those relating to the first clause (John 1:1a); (3) those relating to the second clause (John 1:1b); and, (4) those relating to the third clause (John 1:1c).

(1): Those relating to the verse as a whole (John 1:1). The major question concerning the verse as a whole is one's understanding of the term λογος which appears as the subject in each of the three clauses. Who or what does λογος refer to? And, How is Jesus Christ to be related to or identified with the λογος ? It is interesting that all 15 translations capitalize Word and/or Logos in each clause. Capitalization strongly implies a personal reference. This is especially interesting in the case of #15 where a distinction is suggested between God who is the Word and the revealed forms of Himself in his foreknowledge. Two of these forms are clearly impersonal (the spoken and written forms) and would better be represented by a lower case "word." But the third form, a reference to the incarnate Word, appears clearly to refer to Jesus Christ, who is a person, thus, perhaps, warranting the capitalized "Word." Nevertheless, translation #15 appears to be downplaying the possibility of a pre-existent personal being "with God" in order to avoid the problem of more than one person in the Godhead.

Translations #7 and #13 employ "Logos" rather than "Word," thus preserving the technical term. Translation #13 makes it explicitly clear that this Logos is to be equated with Jesus Christ, using the phrase "Son of God" to clarify this point. Although the author of John's gospel may have understood the λογος to incorporate impersonal and foreknown events, such as the spoken and/or written word, it seems all too clear from 1:14, "the Word became flesh," and the parallels of 1:1 to 1:18, that Jesus Christ is the intended reference.

(2) Those relating to the first clause (John 1:1a). The major problem here has to do with absolute versus relative pre-existence. The question is better stated as one of eternality. Is John telling us that the λογος (which became flesh as Jesus Christ) is eternal? If so, a Trinitarian interpretation finds sup-

port. If not, a Unitarian interpretation finds support. Translations #4 and #12 attempt to stress eternality by their use of "already was." Translation #7 employs "very." Translation #13 actually states that the Logos was "eternally existing." All the other translations are ambiguous on this point. As previously noted (Chapter 3, pages 35-41) ancient Judaism did allow for the creation of certain entities prior to the creation of the world in Genesis 1:1. The question then remains, Does John's gospel help us overcome this ambiguity in any way?

(3) Those relating to the second clause (John 1:1b). The major issue in this clause concerns the personality of the λογος, especially as suggested by the Greek preposition προς. Chapter 2 (pages 30-31) argued for such an understanding. Translations #6 and #9 emphasize this point by departing from the bland "with" to "face to face." Translation #10 utilizes "fellowship." Translation #12 substitutes "dwelt." Translation #13 has "experiencing a face to face fellowship with God the Father," and translation #14 simply states, "in God's presence." In my judgment all of these translations are both faithful to the original Greek and meaningful in contemporary English. Translation #13 does find support in the context of John 1:1-18 for clarifying that "the God" (τον θεον) of 1:1b is to be understood as "God the Father" (see particularly 1:18; this was argued in Chapter 3, page 23).

(4) Those relating to the third clause (John 1:1c). The major difficulty here had to do with the anarthrous θεος (God without the "the"). Chapter 3 (pages 19-23) argued that anarthrous θεος is to be understood in its definite sense (that is to say, as a title for the Supreme Being). Hence, translations #2 ("a god") and #5 and #7 ("divine") are to be rejected (in my judgment, of course). Translations #1, #3, #4, #6, #8, #11, and #14 are to be preferred over #9, #10, #12, and #13 because they simply assert that the "Word was God," without attempting to rule out a functional versus an ontological preference, as do #'s 9, #10, #12, and #13, each in their own way.

To translate is to interpret. Caution is advised in both underinterpreting (as in the interlinear style) and overinterpreting (as in the paraphrase style). Formal equivalent and dynamic equivalent translations are to be recommended, each for different reasons. Often, a combination of these styles makes excellent sense. My own preference for John 1:1 is translation # 1. It is formally equivalent to the Greek text, providing both enough clarity for contemporaray English readers and sufficient ambiguity to force these readers to discern John's intended meaning for themselves from the context.

Conclusion

The focus of this commentary has been on John 1:1 as a prooftext for Trinitarianism or Unitarianism. John 1:1 has been analyzed from several vantage points. The methods of textual, lexical, grammatical, and translation criticism have been explained and applied to our target text. Other methods have been indirectly considered and applied. Since the task of interpretation is ongoing, several more chapters could be written illustrating several other methods. Nevertheless, this commentary comes to a conclusion in this chapter. What follows is a summary of what I see as the pivotal points of interpretation.

Each of the three clauses of John 1:1 contain a crucial issue. In 1:1a, "in the beginning was the Word," the issue concerns the eternality of the Word. In Chapter Three (pages 16-18) I presented three arguments for understanding "in the beginning" in an absolute sense, and three arguments for understanding this phrase in a relative sense. I am more persuaded by the arguments for an absolute sense. Particularly persuasive, to me, is the second argument that I offered (page 17). John 1:3 indicates that the Word was instrumental in the creation of all things, without any apparent exception. This point is emphasized in John 1:3 by the fact that the thought is expressed both positively ("all things were made by Him") and negatively ("and without Him was not any thing made that was made"). Unitarians must argue that the Word Himself (itself) is to be excepted, as the first created being. But, this view, which finds its clearest support from the text of Proverbs 8: 22-24, is suspect for two reasons: (1) the Hebrew words נסך (nasak) and חול (chul), sometimes translated "created" or "made" in Proverbs 8, do not strongly or unambiguously support these translations (cf. Forestell, 1968, 500); and, (2) the atmosphere of Proverbs 8 is poetic and metaphorical. Even if "wisdom" was said to have been "created," it would not have been understood literally. Wisdom is simply a personification of God's immanent presence and creative activity. But,

32

in John 1:1 the Word, which takes on the attributes of Jewish wisdom, is no mere personification. The Word became flesh as the human Jesus, a person clearly distinct from God the Father. The atmosphere of John is realistic and historical/literal.

In 1:1b the main issue concerned the personality of the Word and the relationship that the Word had with God. The preposition $\pi\rho\circ\varsigma$, in my judgement, demands a personal understanding of the Word (see page 13). In addition, verse 18 of the Prologue clarifies that "the God with whom the Word was with" was "the Father." Admittedly, the language of "God the Father," and "God the Son," is neither consistently nor clearly portrayed in the New Testament. Nevertheless, an analysis of John 1:1 in its context lends support to such a distinction (see also 1 John 1:2).

In 1:1c the issue concerned the way in which the Word was predicated as God. In the discussion of this problem I rejected the suggestion that the Word was to be understood as "a god," one of many (see pages 20-22). This suggestion has meager grammatical support and nothing in the context recommends it. Especially persuasive, to me, is the fact that the author of the gospel of John did not choose to use the term $\theta\epsilon\iota\circ\varsigma$, a term which would have made it clear that he understood the Word to be divine, but not deity in any absolute sense. I conclude, therefore, that the title "God" is predicated of the Word in its full and absolute sense.

The term $\lambda\circ\gamma\circ\varsigma$ appears in all three clauses of John 1:1. I find unpersuasive any attempt to distinguish the usage of $\lambda\circ\gamma\circ\varsigma$ from one clause to the next (e.g., as suggested by Wierwille, 1975). It is the same "Word" throughout. This seems abundantly clear from John 1:2 "The same ($\circ\grave{\upsilon}\tau\circ\varsigma$) was in the beginning with God." One of the major difficulties of John's thought, however, is the manner in which he has related the divine Word to the human Jesus. In Christian theology this doctrine is known as the Incarnation. The Word, who was in the beginning (absolutely), who was with God (the Father), and was God (John 1:1), became flesh (John 1:14) as the human person Jesus. The first four centuries of Christianity wrestled with this assertion, coming up with a variety of possible perspectives. Among these were: Docetism; Cerinthianism; Adoptionism; Nestorianism; Apollinarianism; Modalistic Monarchianism; and Arianism (see Grillmeier, *Christ in Christian Tradition*, 1965, for an historical review). The orthodox view settled upon the idea that Jesus was truly God and truly Man, having two natures united in one person (called the hypostatic union). Although I have reasoned that this view finds support from an analysis of John 1:1 in its context, I am aware of several difficulties with this view. These will now be mentioned as items for further study. They could be viewed as concessions to the Unitarian perspective.

First, neither John's gospel nor subsequent orthodox theology has been able to clarify (to the satisfaction of many) how one person can have two natures, one divine, the other human, much less how two natures can co-exist in one person. The category of "mystery" is frequently evoked. One such recent evocation is found in John Polkinghorne's *Quarks, Chaos, and Christianity* (1997): He states:

> "Christians believe that God has shared our lot by living a truly human life in Jesus Christ. This is a tremendous and exciting claim. It means that God has acted to make himself known to us in the plainest possible terms, namely through a human life and a human death. It is also a profoundly mysterious claim. . . its a bit like the physicists with light. . . they knew they had to use both wave language and particle language about it long before they knew how the two could be reconciled. Sometimes one just has to hold on by the skin of one's intellectual teeth. . . " (48).

The last sentence captures the frustration I feel in coming to a Trinitarian conclusion. My readers should appreciate, by now, why I feel compelled to render this verdict in light of the textual, lexical, grammatical, and translation evidence. Yet, it is a verdict that remains troublesome. Unitarians would advocate that I recheck the results of my research and look for ways to "harmonize" John 1:1 with those portions of the New Testament that more clearly differentiate Jesus and God. What Trinitarians call "mysterious," Unitarians call "confusing."

Second, much of contemporary scholarship on John's gospel recognizes stages to the composition of John. Leading scholars in this area posit at least two editions of John's gospel (e.g., Fortna, 1970 & 1988; Nicol, 1972; Teeple, 1974; and, von Wahlde, 1989). The first edition is most often understood as a "signs gospel," centering around the miracles of Jesus. The second edition is understood as an expansion of the "signs gospel" into the gospel as we know it today. This expansion is believed to be have been necessitated by changing circumstances. Those who posit a third edition (e.g., von Wahlde, 1989) simply suggest an additional "necessitating circumstance." Relevant to the research of this commentary is the fact that the earlier editions of the gospel reflect a "low christology," whereas the later editions reflect a "high christology." The former portrays Jesus as a mere man, albeit a prophet; the latter as more than a man, a prophet claiming equality with God. The postulation of two editions to John's gospel provides a basis for explaining either the "mystery," or the "confusion," of one person with two natures. The explanation consists in the recognition that John's gospel set forth a merely human Jesus in its early edition(s), the divine Jesus being a later development. This later development is set forth without any attempt to "solve" the paradox of a divine/human Jesus. The *fact* of the incarnation is asserted; the *manner* of the incarnation remains ambiguous (at least from an explicit biblical perspective). This area of research deserves careful consideration by those wanting further clarity on John 1:1.

Third, the moment of the incarnation remains a problem. Traditionally, the incarnation occurred at the conception, or at the birth of Jesus. This is the Christmas story that Western culture has inherited through orthodox Christianity. God becomes man at Christmas (or nine months previous)! The problem here is that the gospel of John does not appear familiar with either the virginal conception or the infancy stories (unless, of course, one insists upon reading straight across one gospel to the other). According to John 7:40-52 the birth place of Jesus was Nazareth. According to John 1:45 the human father of Jesus was Joseph. According to John 1:1-18, in context with 1:19-34, the moment of the incarnation is the baptism of Jesus! This view is defended at length by Watson (1987, 113-24). In this view the merely human Jesus is "adopted" by the divine Word at his baptism as the chosen instrument of revelation and salvation. This complicates the traditional view of orthodoxy, where the divine and human were joined at conception. Yet, it appears more faithful to the integrity of John's gospel.

Finally, there is the matter of an ontological versus a functional understanding of Jesus as God. As stated in Chapter Three (pages 21-22) John may not have thought of such a distinction. Yet, his readers today are forced to consider these perspectives. In John's first-century world, an agent of someone (called a shaliach) could be addressed *as if he were that person* (functionally), without anyone mistaking for a moment that *he really was that person* (ontologically). This could be the way in which John has portrayed Jesus (argued most persuasively by Harvey, 1982). Unitarians would feel comfortable with this perspective, as it leaves monotheism intact, without any apparent threat of ditheism or tritheism.

But, Jesus is no ordinary shaliach, or agent. John's gospel may have been utilizing a common agency theme from first-century Judaism as a way of talking about Jesus, but one is left with a very extra-ordinary agent. This agent was in the beginning (absolutely) with God (the Father) and was God. This agent created the universe. This agent revealed God. If orthodoxy's maxim that "only God can reveal God," has any merit, and, if Jesus is not fully and ontologically God, then God remains unrevealed! Furthermore, this agent's revelation of God, at its depth, is simultaneously the definitive act of salvation. If this agent reveals God's love and holiness through his self-sacrifice on the cross then, perhaps, this agent is more worthy of our love and worship, at least from a human perspective, than the one who sent him. Afterall, it was the human Jesus who endured the reality of the ordeal! This is consistent with the pattern of messengers and messages in the Ancient Near East. For example, Jerusalem's King Hezekiah, whose city was beseiged by the Assyrian King Sennacherib in 701 B. C. E., sent ". . . all kinds of valuable treasures, his own daughters, concubines, male and female muscians. In order to deliver the tribute and to do obeisance as a slave he sent his personal messenger" (Pritchard, 1969, 288). Greene, in commenting upon the social function of messengers of this type, states, ". . . their social function was to extend humiliation and public embarrassment of the conquered by making it appear that he (the vassal; in this case King Hezekiah) was there in the homeland and capital constantly groveling" (1989, 15). One's sentiments, although somewhat with King Hezekiah, might lean more heavily in the direction of his personal messenger. Likewise, Christians have strong sentiments toward Jesus.

But, evangelical Christians throughout history have had difficulty separating the human from the divine. Their union is proclaimed so beautifully from the hilltop of Calvary. The heart of God and the heart of Jesus seem so indivisibly one. How can Christians worship the one without worshipping the other? Hairsplitting distinctions, such as functional and ontological, appear to fade in the wake of a cross-centered religious experience.

Could it be that John's gospel provides the incipient basis for an innovation upon Jewish monotheism? The orthodox doctrine of the Trinity, although "mysterious," and/or "confusing," appears as the only satisfying resolution to the interpretive demands of "in the beginning was the Word, and the Word was with God, and the Word was God (John 1:1). "

References

Arndt, W. F. & F. W. Gingrich. (1957). *A Greek-English lexicon of the New Testament*. Chicago: University of Chicago.

Barrett, C. K. (1978). *The gospel of John*. Philadelphia: Westminster.

Barrett, C. K. (1987). *The New Testament background: Selected documents*. (revised and expanded version) San Francisco: Harper & Row.

Barth, K. (1986). *Witness to the Word: A commentary on John 1*. Grand Rapids: Eerdmans.

Bauckham, R. J. (1980/81). The worship of Jesus in Apocalyptic Christianity. *New Testament Studies*, 27, 322-41.

Beekman, J. & John Callow. (1974). *Translating the Word of God*. Grand Rapids: Zondervan.

Blass, F. & Albert Debrunner. (1961). *A Greek grammar of the New Testament and other early Christian literature*. (translated by R. W. Funk). Chicago: University of Chicago Press.

Boismard, M. E. (1957). *St. John's prologue*. London: Aquin.

Bolich, G. G. (1986). *The Christian Scholar: An introduction to theological research*. New York: University Press of America.

Boring, E. G., Klaus Berger & Carsten Colpe (Eds.). (1995). *Hellenistic commentary to the New Testament*. Nashville: Abingdon.

Brown, R. E. (1966). *The gospel according to John*. (2 Vols.). Anchor Bible 29, 29A. Garden City: Doubleday.

Bullinger, E. W. (1877). *A critical lexicon and concordance to the English and Greek New Testament*. London: Bagster.

Bullinger, E. W. (1968). *Figures of speech used in the Bible.* Grand Rapids: Baker. (originally published in 1898).

Bultmann, R. (1971). *The gospel of John: A commentary.* Philadelphia: Westminster.

Cartlidge, D. R. & David Dungan. (1980). *Documents for the study of the gospels.* Philadelphia: Fortress.

Collins, J. J. (1997). Jewish monotheism and Christian theology. In Hershel Shanks and Jack Meinhardt (Eds), *Aspects of monotheism: How God is one.* Washington D. C. Biblical Archaelogical Society.

Colwell, E. C. (1933). A definite rule for the use of the article in the Greek New Testament. *Journal of Biblical Literature, 52,* 12-21.

Dana, H. E. & Julius Mantey. (1955). *A manual grammar of the Greek New Testament.* Toronto: MacMillan.

Davies, W. D. (1996). Reflections on aspects of the Jewish background of the gospel of John. In R. A. Culpepper & C. C. Black (Eds.), *Exploring the gospel of John.* (pp. 43-64) Louisville: John Knox.

Debrunner, A. (1967). logo". In G. Kittel & G. Friedrich (Eds.), *Theological dictionary of the New Testament,* Vol. 4. (pp. 69-77). Grand Rapids: Eerdmans.

Delling, G. (1964). ajrch. In G. Kittel & G. Friedrich (Eds.), *Theological dictionary of the New Testament,* Vol. 1. (pp. 478-89). Grand Rapids: Eerdmans.

Dodd, C. H. (1963). *Historical tradition in the fourth gospel.* Cambridge: University.

Dodd, C. H. (1968). *The interpretation of the fourth gospel.* Cambridge: University.

Dunn, J. D. G. (1980). *Christology in the making.* Philadelphia: Westminster.

Erickson, M. J. (1991). *The Word became flesh.* Grand Rapids: Baker.

Finegan, J. (1974). *Encountering New Testament manuscripts: A working introduction to textual criticism.* Grand Rapids: Eerdmans.

Forestell, J. T.. (1968). Proverbs. In R. E. Brown, J. A. Fitzmeyer, & R. E. Murphy, *The Jerome Biblical Commentary.* Englewood Cliffs: Prentice Hall.

Fortna, R. (1970). *The gospel of signs. A reconstruction of the narrative source underlying the fourth gospel.* Cambridge: Cambridge Univ.

Fortna, R. (1988). *The fourth gospel and its predecessor.* Philadelphia: Fortress.

Greene, J. T. (1989). *The role of the messenger and the message in the Ancient Near East.* Brown Judaic Studies 169. Atlanta: Scholars.

Grillmeier, A. (1965). *Christ in Christian tradition.* New York: Sheed & Ward.

Harner, P. B. (1973). Qualitative anarthrous predicate nouns: Mark 15:39 and John 1:1. *Journal of Biblical Literature, 92,* 75-87.

Harris, M. J. (1978). Prepositions & theology in the Greek New Testament. In C. Brown (Ed.), *The new international dictionary of New Testament theology,* Vol. 3. (pp. 1,171-1,215). Exeter: Paternoster.

Harvey, A. E. (1982). *Jesus and the constraints of history.* Philadelphia: Westminster.

Haenchen, E. (1980). *John 1.* Philadelphia: Fortress.

Hoskyns, E. (1947). *The fourth gospel.* London: Faber & Faber.

Kittel, G. & G. Friedrich. (1964-74). *Theological dictionary of the New Testament.* (10 vols., trans. and ed. by G. W. Bromiley). Grand Rapids: Eerdmans.

Kysar, R. (1976). *John: The maverick gospel.* Atlanta: John Knox.

Liddel, H. G., & R. Scott. (1966). *Greek-English lexicon.* Oxford: Oxford University.

Lightfoot, R. H. (1956). *St. John's gospel.* Oxford: Clarendon.

Lindars. B. (1981). *The gospel of John.* New Century Bible. Grand Rapids: Eerdmans.

Lovelady, E. J. (1963). *The logos concept in John 1:1.* Winona Lake: Grace Theological Seminary.

Metzger, B. (1971). *A textual commentary on the Greek New Testament.* New York: United Bible Societies.

Mickelsen, A. B. (1963). *Interpreting the Bible.* Grand Rapids: Eerdmans.

Morris, L. (1971). *The gospel according to John.* New International Commentary on the New Testament. Grand Rapids: Eerdmans.

Moulton, J. H. & G. Milligan. (1930). *The vocabulary of the Greek New Testament.* Grand Rapids: Eerdmans.

Nicol, W. (1972). *The semeia in the fourth gospel.* Leiden: E. J. Brill.

Polkinghorne, J. (1997). *Quarks, Chaos, & Christianity.* New York: Crossroad.

Pollard, T. E. (1958). Cosmology and the purpose of the fourth gospel. *Vigiliae Christianae,* 12, 147-53.

Pritchard, J. B. (Ed.) (1969). *The Ancient Near East: Supplementary texts and pictures relating to the Old Testament.* Princeton: Princeton University.

Reicke, B. (1968). pro". In. G. Kittel & G. Friedrich (Eds.), *Theological dictionary of the New Testament,* Vol. 6. (pp. 720-24). Grand Rapids: Eerdmans.

Roberts, A. J., J. Donaldson, & A. C. Cove (editors). (1926). *The Ante-Nicene Fathers.* 10 Vols. (American reprint of the Edinburgh edition). New York: Scribner's.

Robertson, A. T. (1925). *An introduction to the textual criticism of the New Testament.* Nashville: Broadman.

Robertson, A. T. (1934). *A grammar of the Greek New Testament in light of historical research.* Nashville: Broadman.

Rusch, W. G. (1980). *The Trinitarian controversy.* Philadelphia: Fortress.

Salmon, Victor. (1976). *The fourth gospel: A history of the text.* Collegeville: Liturgical Press.

Schnackenburg, R. (1982). *The gospel according to John.* Vol. 1 (revised edition). New York: Herder & Herder.

Swanson, R. (1995). *New Testament Greek manuscripts: Variant readings arranged in horizontal lines against Codex Vaticanus.* Pasadena: William Carey International University.

Terry, M. S. (1974). *Biblical hermeneutics.* Grand Rapids: Eerdmans.

Teeple, H. M. (1974). *The literary origen of the gospel of John.* Evanston: Religion and Ethics Institute.

Thayer, J. H. (1885). *Thayer's Greek-English lexicon of the New Testament.* Grand Rapids: Baker.

vonWahlde, U. C. (1989). *The earliest version of John's gospel.* Wilmington: Michael Glazier.

Watson, F. (1987). Is John's Christology adoptionistic? In L. D. Hurst & N. T. Wright (Eds.), *The glory of Christ in the New Testament: Studies in honor of G. B. Caird.* New York: Claredon.

Wierwille, V. P. (1975). *Jesus Christ is not God.* New Knoxville: American Christian Press.

Indexes

I. Scripture Reference

II. Subject Index

III. Author Index